NGONI, XHOSA AND SCOT

Published by
Kachere Series
P.O. Box 1037, Zomba, Malawi
ISBN: 978-99908-87-15-0 (Kachere Books no. 22)

Layout and Cover Design: Caroline Chihana

The Kachere Series is represented outside Africa by:
African Books Collective Oxford (orders@africanbookscollective.com)
Michigan State University Press East Lansing (msupress@msu.edu)

Printed by lightning Source

Ngoni, Xhosa and Scot

Religious and Cultural Interaction in Malawi

Jack Thompson

Kachere Books no. 22

Kachere Series
Zomba
2007

*To my friends **Matiya Nkhoma**, at whose invitation I delivered three of the lectures in this book and **Boston Soko**, with whom I share a fascination with Ngoni origins and history.*

Kachere Series
P.O. Box 1037, Zomba, Malawi
Email: kachere@globemw.net
www.kachereseries.org

This book is part of the Kachere Series, a range of books on religion, culture and society from Malawi. Some related Kachere titles published so far are:

John McCracken, *Politics & Christianity in Malawi 1875-1940: The Impact of the Livingstonia Mission in the Northern Province*

T. Cullen Young: *Missionary and Anthropologist*

Margaret Sinclair, *Salt and Light: The Letters of Jack and Mamie Martin in Malawi 1921-28*

Orison Ian Mkandawire, *Chiswakhata Mkandawire of Livingstonia*

Yesaya Zerenji Mwasi, *Essential and Paramount Reasons for Working Independently*

Martin Pauw, *Mission and Church in Malawi: A History of the Nkhoma Synod of the Church of Central Africa Presbyterian 1889-1962*

Isabel Apawo Phiri, *Women, Presbyterianism and Patriarchy: Religious Experience of Chewa Women in Central Malawi*

Andrew C. Ross, *Blantyre Mission and the Making of Modern Malawi*

Jurgens Johannes van Wyk, *The Historical Development of the Offices according to the Presbyterian Tradition of Scotland*

Steven Paas, *Ministers and Elders: The Birth of Presbyterianism*

The Kachere Series is the publications arm of the Department of Theology and Religious Studies of the University of Malawi

Series Editors: J.C. Chakanza, Chimwemwe Katumbi, F.L. Chingota, Klaus Fiedler, P.A. Kalilombe, Martin Ott, Shareef Mahommad

Contents

Foreword

This collection of essays and lectures by Jack Thompson, entitled *Ngoni, Xhosa and Scot: Religious and Cultural Interaction in Malawi*, provides an extraordinarily rich resource for people interested in the history of Malawi. It shines a bright light not only on the planting and growth of Christianity in the Northern Region of Malawi but also on the Ngoni people, their role in that story and in the history of Malawi in the late nineteenth and early twentieth centuries. It also illustrates the complicated interaction of Scottish missionaries in the Cape with the Xhosa people and with the Scottish missionaries in Malawi and the people of Malawi. This is not limited to the distant past: important and vital Malawi/South African interaction has continued in a variety of forms until today and requires much more attention by Malawi historians than it has received so far. These essays are a foundation stone for this development.

The essays are also an illustration of the way historians to-day have been able to expand the range of resources available to aid the understanding of the past. In the essay entitled, *Xhosa Missionaries to Malawi: Identity and Photography*, Jack's use of photographs as a tool for understanding the past and not simply as a source of illustrations for books, is a classic example of this expansion in the use of resources.

As a pastor among the southern Ngoni of Nkosi Gomani I used to love to sing with the people the setting to the tune of an Ngoni victory song, of the hymn *Khondoyo yatha ... The Strife is o'er*. This joyous triumphant setting transforms the whole impact of the hymn from that made by the English version and its setting. Deeply interested in traditional hymnody I had always assumed that the astonishing flowering of indigenous hymnody in Northern Malawi, which, through translation into chiNyanja from siNgoni and chiTumbuka, is now a gift to all Malawians and many Zambians, was due to the initiative of Donald Fraser. The essay on William Koyi shows how the keystones were laid by Koyi, with the help of his friend, John Knox Bokwe, the great hymn-writer and composer of the amaXhosa. It was on this foundation that Donald Fraser had the imagination to encourage, build up and expand what became the rich heritage of indigenous hymnody of Northern Malawi produced by Ngoni, Tumbuka and Tonga.

These essays make clear that the development of a Christian culture in Northern Malawi was the product of the interaction of Scot, Xhosa, Ngoni, Tonga and Tumbuka. There were no 'passive recipients of cultural imperialism'. This was despite the fact that some Scots missionaries of that period saw Africans simply as recipients of a new culture and religion with nothing to give, just as some critics of missions in the last decades of the twentieth century also insult African people by writing of them as if they had been the 'passive victims' of that imperialism.

I was delighted to be asked to write a foreword to this stimulating series of essays by Jack, successively my student, my colleague and then my successor, and always my friend.

Andrew C. Ross
New College
University of Edinburgh

Black Strangers or Fellow Countrymen? Early Xhosa Missionaries to Malawi

Livingstone and Lovedale

In 1841 two unconnected events (at the time seemingly unimportant, and linked only by their connections to Scotland and missions) took place in South Africa. The first was the arrival of David Livingstone at the beginning of his missionary career in Africa; the second was the opening in the Tyumie valley in the eastern Cape of the Lovedale educational institution.[1]

During the next thirty-three years these two very different examples of Scottish missionary initiative went their own separate ways—Livingstone becoming perhaps the most famous of all nineteenth century missionaries to Africa, Lovedale building up a reputation as possibly the best educational institution in Africa south of the equator. It was only after the death of Livingstone that (metaphorically speaking) their paths were to cross.

When, in April 1874, Livingstone's remains were interred in Westminster Abbey, one of those present at the funeral was Dr. James Stewart, the principal of Lovedale. In earlier years, before becoming principal of Lovedale, Stewart had had connections with Livingstone, for in 1861 as an enthusiastic young theological student, he had approached the Free Church of Scotland about funding an expedition to the area of the Zambezi and the Shire highlands (in what is now Malawi) to investigate the possibilities of the region as a site for a mission to Central Africa.[2] When the Free Church refused to fund the venture, Stewart raised the money from a group of interested industrialists and businessmen, not only in Edinburgh and Glasgow, but also in Liverpool and Manchester as well. The basis on which the proposed mission was to be founded was described as follows:

> The principle on which the mission is proposed to be founded is that of making it as speedily as possible self-supporting. And this is to be attempted by introducing other labourers than ordained ministers and teachers. There seems

---

[1] Lovedale had opened as a station of the Glasgow Missionary Society in 1820, but it was only in 1841 that the educational institution, with which the name was later associated, came into being.

[2] An account of these events was later given by Stewart himself in *Livingstonia: its Origin*, Edinburgh, 1894, chapter 1, 'First Efforts', 1-16.

9

to be a felt necessity that a direct and open effort should be made to follow up the labours of missionaries by industrial and civilising appliances.[3]

It should be noted here that the self-sufficiency of which Stewart wrote was not so much based on Henry Venn's 'three-self' principles, as on Livingstone's ideas of the civilising colony, and was to be produced by mission-generated industry, agriculture and trade, overseen by skilled artisans.

The above principles were contained in a statement which Stewart's committee drew up—together with a list of questions which were to be sent to Livingstone, concerning the suitability of the area for missionary work. The document contained another interesting statement. Though Stewart was later to become principal of Lovedale—a post he held for thirty-five years until his death in 1905—he had not, at this time, any direct experience of that institution. Yet the statement of purpose for the proposed mission contained the following paragraph on probable staffing:

> Of the number of missionaries sent out—whether two, three or four—one, and in all probability two, will be fully qualified as medical men, in addition, as is expected, to their being regularly ordained ministers of the Free Church. These will be accompanied by two European, or three native African artisans, if, as is probable, the industrial department of the Free Church at Lovedale in Kaffraria can furnish such men.[4]

It is, of course, possible that the suggestion to include artisans from Lovedale originated with one of the other members of the committee. Whether or not this was the case, the possibility had taken root in Stewart's mind—though it was to be another fifteen years before he was actually able to put it into practice. Stewart travelled out to Africa with Mary Livingstone, on her way back to meet her husband after many years of separation and misery in Britain. A friendship quickly grew between the young man and the older woman. By this period, Mary Livingstone had become dependent on alcohol as a result of her loneliness, and was also having doubts about her own Christian faith. Stewart—a doctor and a Christian minister—seems to have been able to help her with both problems.[5] By the time Stewart reached the Zambezi, he had developed a distinctly negative view of Livingstone and his efforts—a view which was only reinforced by the periods he spent with Livingstone in 1862 and 1863. By the time that he and Livingstone parted in January 1863 Stewart wrote that 'I part with Dr. L., and have no wish what-

[3] *Ibid.* 10

[4] *Ibid.*

[5] Stewart kept very detailed journals during this period. They are held as Stewart Papers, National Archives of Zimbabwe, Harare. Parts of his journal have been published as J.P.R. Wallis (ed.), *The Zambesi Journal of James Stewart*, London, 1952.

ever to meet him again. Bad faith and insincerity will always come out.'[6] A few weeks later Stewart recorded a much more extravagant gesture in his journal:

> In the afternoon I went down to the river bank a short way and threw with all my strength into the torpid muddy weed-covered Zambesi my copy of certain 'Missionary Travels in South Africa'. The volume was fragrant with odours of and memories of the earnestness with which I studied the book in days gone by. How different it appeared now! It was nothing short of an eyesore, the very sight of its brown covers. I do not think it is, as the Rev. R- M-[7] is said to have called it, 'a pack of lies', but it would need a great many additions to make it the truth. Thus I disliked the book and sent it to sink or swim into the vaunted Zambesi. So perish all that is false in myself and others.[8]

On his return to Scotland, Stewart recommended that the time was not right for the setting up a mission in the area, and nothing was done about it for the next eleven years.

Lovedale and Livingstonia

By the time of Livingstone's funeral in 1874, however, Stewart's views had mellowed considerably. He was, by then, the principal of Lovedale, home on leave when Livingstone's remains arrived back in Britain. Stewart attended the funeral in Westminster Abbey in April, and, following it travelled north to the General Assembly of the Free Church of Scotland, and proposed the setting up of a mission in Livingstone's memory, to be called Livingstonia.[9] Though the Free Church welcomed the proposal, as with Stewart's expedition in 1861, it was actually financed, not by the Foreign Missions Committee, but by a committee of interested individuals—many of them prosperous Glasgow industrialists. Stewart himself would have been keen to lead the expedition, but he was urgently required back at Lovedale, and when the pioneer party set out in mid-1875 it was led by E.D. Young, another veteran of Central African travel,[10] who was seconded from his naval duties, and chosen for his seamanship, as the party took with it the steamer *Ilala*, built at Millwall, but carried out in seven hundred pieces, and re-assembled on the Shire river. Within a year, however, Stewart was to renew his direct connection with the mission, when he led a second party

---

[6] *Ibid.*, l0th January 1863
[7] I.e., Robert Moffatt, Livingstone's father-in-law.
[8] *Ibid.,* 1st February 1863.
[9] Stewart, *Livingstonia: its Origin*, 44-48.
[10] Young had been a member of Livingstone's Zambezi expedition, and had led the Livingstone search expedition to lake Malawi in 1867.

from the Eastern Cape to Malawi—a party which included four Xhosa evangelists, chosen from fourteen volunteers at Lovedale. The Lovedale Institution to which Stewart returned in 1875 was a far cry from the single tutor and twenty pupils which had made up its entire complement when it opened in 1841. By the mid-1870s it had expanded to a college of almost five hundred pupils—male and female, black and white, involved in a whole range of courses which varied from logic, moral philosophy and political economy, through home economics to carpentry, printing, and wagon-making, and with a staff of more than twenty.[11] Some idea of how the directors of the Lovedale Institution saw their task may be gleaned by quoting from the first annual report—an innovation which was begun after the 1872 session. On the opening page of this first report Stewart laid out the 'Objects of the Institution'. They make interesting reading.

> First: To train as preachers such young men as may be found intellectually and spiritually to fit such work.
>
> Second: To train teachers for native schools.
>
> Third: To train a certain number in the various arts of printing, wagonmaking, black-smithing, carpentering, bookbinding, general agricultural work, and a few as telegraphic clerks.
>
> Fourth: To give a general education to those whose course in life is not yet decided.
>
> Above all, as is implied in the name Missionary Institution, we seek that those under our care may become the subjects of that great change–genuine conversion to God. Without this we do not regard all the other results as of the highest value. They are worthy of effort, but our greatest anxiety is to see those who are here exhibiting the true and practical fruits of the Christian life.[12]

Once again we see at work the philosophy of the industrial mission, with the inculcation of the dignity of hard manual labour. Even when we come to the definition of the missionary nature of the institution, it is clear that the primary understanding here was not to train indigenous missionaries for other parts of the country (or indeed, the continent) but to bring about the evangelical conversion of the pupils at the school. The development of the Livingstonia mission 1500 miles further north, was, however, to afford an opportunity for a change in (or at least a development of) that philosophy. As we have seen, the idea of using Lovedale graduates as missionaries to

---

[11] R.H. W. Shepherd, *Lovedale South Africa: the Story of a Century, 1841-1941*, 64; and Lovedale Annual Report, 1876.

[12] Lovedale Annual Report, 1872, 3.

Malawi had begun in the mind of Stewart (or his original 1861 committee) fifteen years earlier. Now, in a letter to Stewart, written from Cape Maclear, on the southern shores of Lake Malawi, where the pioneer mission party had set up their headquarters in October 1875, Robert Laws, the young second in command of the party, called for recruits from the eastern Cape. He wrote, 'we have a splendid field here for native catechists or men from Lovedale. In a short time we shall be ready for them.'[13] Stewart immediately used the letter as an opportunity to call for recruits for the new mission. On 29th May 1876 he called together the senior pupils of the school, and read the letter to them, before asking for volunteers.[14] Fourteen were immediately forthcoming (though one quickly withdrew again). Of these, four were eventually chosen early in June, and, in little more than a month were on their way to Central Africa.

Several points are of interest in this process. The first is that, unlike the proposal of 1861, the call for volunteers was not limited to artisans. The report of the meeting which Stewart called (actually a series of three meetings held on 29th and 30th May) records that 'fourteen in all offered their services in different capacities as evangelists, teachers and tradesmen.'[15] The second is that among those volunteering were some of Lovedale's finest products of the period. They included both Mpambani Mzimba and Elijah Makiwane, the first two Africans to be ordained in South Africa as Presbyterian ministers, as well as John Knox Bokwe, who, over the next half century was to go on to become one of the most outstanding graduates and servants of Lovedale in the whole of its history. None of these was chosen. It was considered that they were too important to the work of the church in South Africa, to be risked in the uncertainty of a pioneer mission to Central Africa.[16] Instead the four chosen were what we might call middle-rankers. They were William Koyi, Shadrach Mngunana, Isaac Williams Wauchope, and Mapassa Ntintili. Of these two, Williams and Mngunana went as teachers, Koyi as a general handyman, and Ntintili as a carpenter .

Thus began what was, at the time, sometimes referred to as 'an experiment': using indigenous Africans as missionaries in other parts of Africa to work alongside, but under the control of Scottish missionaries. Altogether it lasted for twelve years—a period by no means free from controversy—either between the Xhosa and the Scots, or between the Scots themselves, as to the

---

[13] *Christian Express*, 1ˢᵗ June 1876, 1.

[14] *Ibid.*, 2.

[15] *Ibid.*

[16] *The Lovedale News*, 16ᵗʰ June 1876, 2.

nature and success of the undertaking. It was not, of course, unique—there were similar indigenous undertakings in several other parts of Africa. Nevertheless, it was, I believe, of sufficient interest and significance to engage out attention, even over a century and a quarter later.

The Xhosa Missionaries in Malawi: an Outline

It might here be useful to give a brief outline of the main events of the undertaking, to set it in its context before looking at some of the main issues which it raised: not least that of the identity of the Xhosa missionaries themselves—who did they perceive themselves to be in this new context, and how did the other players in the drama (the Scottish missionaries and the Ngoni people of northern Malawi) view them?

The four Lovedale volunteers (together with Stewart himself, and a party of around twenty—including new recruits not only for the Livingstonia mission, but also for the Blantyre mission of the Church of Scotland) set out from Port Elizabeth on 27th July 1876,[17] and eventually reached Lake Malawi in October. Even before reaching their destination one of the four, Isaac Wauchope, had been struck by severe and recurrent fever which took the form, not simply of lassitude, but of mental delusions, and periodic violence. Within a couple of months of his arrival Stewart took the decision to send him back to South Africa, commenting that, 'since 2nd September he has been useless'[18] That Wauchope went on to make a full recovery, and to have an important and interesting career in South Africa is, unfortunately, something which cannot detain us in this particular paper, but which I have written about elsewhere.[19] His illness did, however, shatter one of the myths of using African evangelists in the Livingstonia mission—that they would be better able than Europeans to stand up to the rigours of a tropical climate. Within the next few months, the death, first of all of Dr. William Black (who had travelled north with Stewart's party) and then of Shadrach Mngunana (probably the most able of the Lovedale volunteers) emphasised that both

---

[17] Isaac Williams [Wauchope] to Mr. Smith, Quelimane, 15th August 1876, published in *Christian Express*, 1st November 1876, 10.

[18] Stewart to Alexander Duff, Livingstonia, 4th December 1876, Ms. 7876, Livingstonia Papers, National Library of Scotland.

[19] A full account of Wauchope's subsequent career as political activist, temperance campaigner, Xhosa poet, amateur historian, Christian minister and proponent of African higher education appears in my book, *Touching the Heart: Xhosa Missionaries to Malawi 1876-1888*, chapter 8, 163-194. He was drowned when the troopship *Mendi* sank in the English Channel during the First World War.

Europeans and Xhosa members were equally susceptible to the ravages of the Malawi climate.

Within a year of arriving at Cape Maclear, therefore, the Xhosa missionaries had been reduced from four to two. Moreover (in professional and academic terms at least) the two remaining, Koyi and Ntintili, were much less able than those who had gone. Nevertheless, over the next few years, both men made useful and important contributions to the beginnings of Christianity in Malawi. Though Ntintili was trained as a carpenter and wagon maker, he also acted as a school teacher, and spent more than a year and a half helping out at the Church of Scotland mission at Blantyre which, in the first few years of its existence was on the verge of collapse, due mainly to unsuitable staff, and depended on help from Livingstonia just to survive.[20] Ntintili's part in this exercise has been consistently undervalued in studies of this period.

William Koyi's contribution to the early days of the Livingstonia mission has received more attention.[21] He soon became an indispensable part of the many journeys of exploration which the missionaries and their associates (such as the brothers Moir, founders of the African Lakes Corporation) undertook. His linguistic ability became particularly important as the missionaries made contact with various groups of the Ngoni people, who had migrated from South Africa in the 1820s and who spoke an Nguni language very similar to Koyi's mother tongue, Xhosa. In addition, however, he acted as a *capitao* on several of the journeys, and probably became the first outsider in modern times to discover coal in Malawi.[22] (His subsequent importance will be dealt with briefly later in the paper).

Both Koyi and Ntintili remained in Malawi until 1880, when they returned to the Cape on leave. Both had intended to marry and then return to Malawi for a further period of service. In the event Mapassa Ntintili never went back. This was due partly to Laws' reservations about his effectiveness, and partly to long delays brought about by Stewart's unwillingness to let the

---

[20] See Andrew C. Ross, *Blantyre Mission and the Making of Modern Malawi*, Blantyre, Malawi, 1996. 18-21 and 43-49.

[21] For example, in classic missionary works such as W.P. Livingstone's *Laws of Livingstonia*, W.A. Elmslie's *Among the Wild Ngoni*, and, more recently, in John McCracken's *Politics and Christianity in Malawi*, and T. Jack Thompson's *Christianity in Northern Malawi*, and *Touching the Heart*.

[22] Robert Laws, 'Journey along part of the western side of lake Nyassa in 1878' in *Proceedings of the Royal Geographical Society*, vol. 1, 1879, 312.

Xhosa evangelists return until a new, more healthy headquarters had been chosen for the mission.

William Koyi returned at the end of 1881. Though he had married, his wife (the second daughter of Rev. Andries van Rooyen)[23] did not join him until near the end of 1884. From just after his return until his death from tuberculosis in June 1886 Koyi worked at Njuyu, among the northern Ngoni. I have written about the pioneering significance of this work elsewhere.[24] Suffice it to say here that even to-day, nearly one hundred and twenty years after his death, Koyi is remembered and respected in northern Malawi. As pioneer missionary , interpreter of language, religion and culture, and trusted adviser of both Scottish missionaries and Ngoni chiefs, his place in the history of Malawian Christianity is assured.

While Koyi was still working at Njuyu, the last of the Lovedale evangelists, George Williams (no relation of Isaac Williams Wauchope) arrived at Bandawe (the new headquarters of the mission) at Christmas 1883.[25] He was soon posted to Ngoni country , where he worked, both alongside Koyi, and, later, at the newly opened sub-station of Chinyera. By this time Koyi had been joined by the Scots missionary Walter Angus Elmslie, and the latter and Williams never got on together. Before Williams tour had finished, Elmslie sent an ultimatum to Laws, threatening that if Williams was re-appointed, he would resign from the mission.[26] When Williams returned to the Cape in 1888 he was not re-appointed, and with his departure ended the use of Lovedale-trained Xhosa personnel in Malawi. While in my own mind there is little doubt that they contributed significantly to the beginnings of the Livingstonia mission, contemporary missionary verdicts were much more ambivalent—regarding the experiment, at best, as a very qualified success, and, at worst, as a distinct failure.

The whole undertaking, lasting as it did for twelve years and involving the death in Malawi of two of the five participants, and the serious illness of a third, deserves serious consideration. In the remainder of the paper I shall attempt to answer several questions about the episode. Was there an underlying policy behind it? How did the Scots regard the Xhosa missionaries?

---

[23] I regret that in spite of considerable efforts, I have been unable so far to find any reference to her personal name in any of the sources.

[24] See 'William Koyi and the Ngoni' in this book.

[25] Bandawe Journal, 24th December 1883, Ms. 7911, Livingstonia Papers, NLS.

[26] Elmslie to Laws, Njuyu, Angoniland, 18th September 1888, Livingstonia Papers, National Archives of Malawi, Zomba.

How did the Xhosa themselves understand their own role, and their identity vis à vis the Scottish missionaries, and the indigenous peoples of Malawi?

A Missionary Policy on the Use of Xhosa Evangelists?

In spite of the fact that the idea of using Xhosa evangelists trained at Lovedale can be dated back to 1861 (as we have seen) there seems to have been no clearly thought-out policy with regard to them. This is indicated by several events. The first is the uncertainty about how much to pay them, and how and where they fitted into the somewhat hierarchical mission structure in terms of ordained ministers and/or doctors, qualified teachers, and artisans. To begin with, most of them were better educated than many of the Scottish artisans. While it is true that they would have started school at a much later age than their Scottish counterparts, it is also the case that, in some cases, they continued much longer, and undertook a range of subjects (based closely on the Scottish syllabus in any case) which the less well-educated of their Scottish colleagues would not have tackled. This difference can be seen clearly in the letters that each group wrote. The best educated of the Xhosa men wrote at a level of literacy and fluency which was far above that of many of the Scottish artisans. Even the less educated Xhosa—Koyi and Ntintili—wrote letters in English of at least as high a literary standard as some of their Scottish artisan colleagues.

How, if at all, was this position reflected in the comparative level of salaries paid to the two groups? When the four Xhosa volunteers came to Malawi in 1876 they were paid £45 per year (plus rations).[27] This was approximately half of the salary of a Scottish artisan. On the other hand, it was approximately the same salary that the first black ministers from Lovedale, Mpambani Mzimba and Elijah Makiwane—both, of course, rejected volunteers for Livingstonia in 1876—were paid to look after their congregations in the Eastern Cape.[28] To some extent it was this level, rather than any comparison with Scottish salaries, which determined how much the Xhosa evangelists were paid, for clearly, it would have been very difficult to pay them at a level in excess of what their ordained colleagues were getting in the Cape. Thus it would probably be true to say that it was racial differentials in South Africa which determined the rate at which the Xhosa missionaries were remunerated. Several years later, when William Koyi returned to Malawi for a second period of service, he reached a top salary of

---

[27] Stewart to Smith, 28th April 1880, Ms. 7876, Livingstonia Papers, NLS.
[28] Ibid., Stewart to Duff, 14th February 1877.

£130 per annum[29] approximately the same as that for an equivalent Scottish artisan.

A second question was that of how the Xhosa evangelists actually related to the mission in terms of employment. This can be illustrated by an incident which occurred in August 1877 when Stewart, concerned about the unhealthiness of the mission site, wrote an official letter to Alexander Duff and the Livingstonia committee in Scotland. This letter was ostensibly signed by all the members of the Livingstonia staff, and began:

> Rev. and Dear Sir, We the members of the Livingstonia Mission beg respectfully to express to the Foreign Missions Committee our unanimous conviction that the present site of the mission is, from a variety of causes, quite unsuitable. Its chief and only recommendation is its possession of a good harbour. We think, therefore, that a more suitable site should at least be sought for— whether it can be found or should be finally selected, as the permanent position or not.[30]

While written by Stewart, this was a letter claiming to be sent (and signed) by all the members of the mission. Yet the signatures of neither Koyi nor Ntintili appear on the letter. All the Scottish staff of the mission, including the artisans, have signed it. In general, as McCracken points out, the Lovedale evangelists were regarded as members of the staff, rather than servants of the mission,[31] and indeed, their names appear in various places, such as the Livingstonia staff book, and other official lists of staff. It is all the more surprising then, that a letter written just a few weeks after the death of Shadrach Mngunana, and almost certainly partly initiated by that death, should have omitted the signatures of his two Xhosa colleagues. Mapassa Ntintili was at Blantyre, rather than at Cape Maclear, but contact between the two stations was regular, and it would not have been difficult to ensure that a letter, largely drawing its appeal from the fact that it represented the unanimous views of the staff, actually contained all their signatures. The conclusion seems inescapable that the decision to omit the Xhosa signatures was deliberate; and if that were the case, it can have been based on nothing other than racial grounds.

Further complicating the situation, was the undoubted rivalry between Stewart and Laws—especially after Stewart had returned to Lovedale early in 1878. Following Stewart's return to South Africa, Laws became the leader

---

[29] Minutes of the Livingstonia committee, 24th December 1885, Ms. 7912, NLS.

[30] The Members of the Livingstonia Mission to Rev. Dr. Duff, Convenor of the Foreign Mission Committee, Edinburgh; Livingstonia, 6th August 1877, Ms. 7876, Livingstonia Papers, NLS.

[31] John McCracken, *Politics and Christianity in Malawi*, 190.

of the mission (and was to remain so for the next fifty years). Stewart, on the other hand, regarded himself as the founder of the mission (as is made particularly clear in his book *Livingstonia: its Origin*) and always retained a somewhat patriarchal (not to say proprietorial) attitude towards it. In addition, as principal of Lovedale, he felt a particular responsibility for the Lovedale graduates working at Livingstonia.

This rivalry reached its climax during the time when Koyi and Ntintili were back in South Africa, at the end of their first tour of duty. As has been indicated above, Stewart had had doubts about the site of Livingstonia for some time,[32] situated as it was at the southern end of the lake, in what, even to-day, is a very inaccessible spot, except by sea. In addition, the site was unhealthy, had a very limited population, and very little arable land. In spite of several appeals for a change of site no move had been made. While Koyi and Ntintili were preparing to return, news reached Lovedale of the death of John Gunn, one of the Scottish artisans. This was the last straw for Stewart. He refused to allow any of the Lovedale evangelists to return until a new site had been chosen.[33] It was to be well over a year later before Koyi actually returned, by which time Bandawe had been named as the new headquarters of the mission. Mapassa Ntintili, however, had already taken up work as a teacher in the Transkei, and was never to return to Malawi. While there was much of the plain common sense in Stewart's attitude, it also smacked of the patriarchal, and was made much more sustainable by the absence of a clear-cut policy on the precise relationship of the Lovedale evangelists to the mission.[34]

Had the experiment continued for a longer period some coherent policy might have emerged from the Livingstonia committee in Scotland. As it was, the pioneering nature, not only of the mission enterprise itself, but of the use of Xhosa evangelists in it, meant that, by and large, the committee was largely, if not wholly, dependent on the views and advice of returning missionaries. This was particularly the case with regard to salaries for the evangelists. On the whole, the committee in Scotland were inclined to suggest lower salaries than the missionaries, such as Stewart and Laws were sug-

---

[32] He had expressed doubts about the site within a few days of first arriving at Cape Maclear. See Dr. Stewart to Rev. Buchanan, Livingstonia, Lake Nyassa, 26th October 1876, published in *Christian Express*, 1st February 1877, 4-5.

[33] Stewart to Secretary of the Livingstonia Committee, 18th August 1880, Ms. 7876, Livingstonia Papers, NLS.

[34] That is to say, to whom were they responsible, and who could control their movements? If they had been members of the mission in the full sense, their return would have been decided by the Livingstonia committee, rather than Stewart.

gesting. At their meeting of 22nd July 1880, for example, the committee expressed the view that a salary of £80-90 per annum (plus rations) which had been suggested for Koyi and Ntintili if they returned as married men, was too high.[35] By their meeting of 4th April 1881, however, and following a letter from Laws, they had agreed to £100.[36] (Lest it be thought that such haggling was based merely on race, it might be pointed out that this amount was more than was being suggested for a female Scottish teacher who was recruited at the same time.)[37]

On one occasion the committee expressed a very specific opinion on the relationship between black and white missionaries. Stewart, in a letter read to the committee on 28th June 1881, suggested that, rather than young and inexperienced evangelists from Lovedale, more experienced men should be sent. He suggested specifically that Rev. Mpambani Mzimba (one of those who had originally volunteered in 1876, and who was still keen to go to Malawi) should be sent. The committee accepted the proposal, but added the directive 'Mr. Mzimba should occupy a subordinate position to Dr. Laws and be wholly under his authority'.[38] In doing so, they were merely confirming what was clearly the practice of the mission already, though the need for clarity was obviously based on Mzimba's theoretically equal ecclesiastical status to Laws.

Xhosa Identity in Malawi

This leads us to one of the most intriguing questions of this whole period: how the Xhosa evangelists themselves saw their identity vis à vis the Scottish missionaries on the one hand, and the peoples of Malawi on the other, and how they, in turn, were perceived by the other groups with and among whom they worked. Many clues to this emerge in the first days of their service with the Livingstonia mission—indeed even on the journey to Malawi itself. The Xhosa evangelists were copious letter-writers at this time, writing both to their ex-teachers, and to their friends at Lovedale, and their letters (or extracts from them) appeared in the press in both English and Xhosa. One can detect in these early letters a mixture of excitement and uncertainty, and already, in some of them, a feeling of isolation. For all of the Xhosa evangelists this would have been their first trip out of the Cape, and, though they

---

[35] Minutes of the Livingstonia committee, 22nd July 1880, Ms. 7912, NLS.

[36] Ibid., 4th April 1881.

[37] Ibid., 2nd June 1880 and 10th January 1881.

[38] Ibid., 28th June 1881. In practice Mzimba never came to Malawi, as the Lovedale Presbytery refused him permission to go.

were only two weeks sailing from Port Elizabeth, so much appeared new and strange to them. The languages of the area they found fascinating—trying to make connections with their own Xhosa tongue, yet struggling with pronunciation and intonation.[39] Their reactions to the people were paradoxical: on the one hand writing that 'their state, both socially and morally is pitiable',[40] on the other, identifying with them and describing them as 'these our countrymen'.[41] On occasion, both attitudes appear in the same sentence, as when Shadrach Mngunana, writing of the arrival at Cape Maclear of a group of people fleeing from slave traders, speaks of 'my poor and most pitiable countrymen'.[42]

In these early days their relationship to the Scots missionaries was also somewhat uncertain. In one sense they were colleagues; on the other hand (and particularly in the presence of Stewart) they were, in most cases, recently graduated pupils, working alongside their principal. One good example of this uncertain relationship occurred soon after their arrival at Cape Maclear. E.D. Young, because of his naval service, and his previous experience in Central Africa, had been selected to lead the first party in 1875, see the *Ilala* safely re-assembled and sailed into Lake Malawi, and choose a site for the mission. It had never been expected that he would stay more than a year or two, and, with the arrival of Stewart in October 1876, the time seemed right for him to leave. A farewell dinner was held in his honour. On this occasion Shadrach Mngunana and William Koyi acted as waiters for the Scottish missionaries.[43] In many ways this occasion sums up the slightly uneasy social relationship which persisted between the Scots and the Xhosa. In some respects they were colleagues, occupying the same space, and doing the same job; in others they were still in a master-servant relationship.

In a letter back to Lovedale, Shadrach Mngunana, commenting on the farewell dinner, and their role as waiters, wrote, 'I was reminded of our old dear Lovedale, which we hope to see again if God spares us'.[44] The tone of

---

[39] Isaac Williams [Wauchope] to Mr. Smith, Quelimane, 15th August 1876, in *Christian Express*, 1st November 1876, 10.

[40] Shadrach Mngunana to Mr. Macdonald, 29th November 1876, in *Lovedale News*, 8th March 1877, 1.

[41] Isaac Williams [Wauchope] to Mr. Smith, 15th August 1876, in *Lovedale News*, 25th October 1876, 2.

[42] Shadrach Mngunana to the Editor of *The Lovedale News*, 15th June 1877, 2.

[43] Shadrach Mngunana to Mr. Macdonald, 29th November 1876, in *Lovedale News*, 8th March 1877, 2.

[44] Ibid.

the comments indicates no discomfort or resentment at this particular relationship (though it has to be said that it was written to one of the Scots missionaries at Lovedale). This would seem to indicate that such roles were normal at Lovedale, where, of course, there would be no question of a social equality between the races—and certainly not between teacher and pupil. This perception of difference, though slightly diluted by distance, essentially remained intact in Central Africa, except, to some extent, when just two missionaries—one white, one black—were working together in an isolated situation, when the social conventions of the day might sometimes be relaxed. In general, however, the Xhosa evangelists were treated with something like the same distance that a teacher might adopt towards a prefect in a Victorian school.

In this situation of uncertainty (with regard to their relationships both with local peoples and with the Scots missionaries) the Xhosa evangelists naturally depended on each other a great deal. In particular, Wauchope, Mngunana and Ntintili began to regard Koyi as a confidant and adviser. This may seem a little odd, given the fact that, in comparison, at least, to Mngunana and Wauchope, he was of fairly limited education; but there were more important factors at work. Koyi at this time was around thirty years of age. The other Xhosa evangelists were all his juniors. While Ntintili was only a couple of years younger than Koyi, both Mngunana and Wauchope were considerably younger—twenty-three and twenty-four respectively. In spite of his limited education, William Koyi had been very well respected at Lovedale, and, in the double strangeness and uncertainty of a new culture and a new relationship with the Europeans of the party (in which the Xhosa evangelists were never entirely sure where they stood) Koyi's maturity and steadiness were reassuring. Writing back to Lovedale at this time, Isaac Wauchope made clear the close relationship which was beginning to develop between the Xhosa evangelists, and, in particular, Koyi' s central place in it:

> We are all well yet, and hope to be spared to the end. We love one another very much and there are no quarrels among us. We are still looking forward without any doubts and expect to face all difficulties like men. William Koyi is like a father to us, and we are like sons to him.[45]

Later, after Wauchope had been sent back to the Cape and Mngunana had died, Ntintili expressed similar sentiments about Koyi. At a point where Koyi was away on a journey of exploration, Ntintili wrote back to friends at Lovedale '1 feel the want of my brother Koyi', and on various other

---

[45] Isaac Williams [Wauchope] to Mr. Bennie, no date, in *Lovedale News*, 25th October 1876, 8

occasions referred to Koyi as 'my brother'.[46] Undoubtedly the most telling comment, however, on the relationship of the Xhosa evangelists with both Scots missionaries and local tribes, comes in a letter which William Koyi wrote to Mapassa Ntintili during his first visit to the southern Ngoni in 1878. It survives only in published form, and, in the light of its contents it seems rather odd that it has escaped the editorial pen of the missionary editor of the *Christian Express*. Writing of his visit to Chikuse's village, Koyi told his friend,

> If then, I am spared to return, I fear I will leave you at Livingstonia, for though I may be nothing there, I am recognised as something here! I found brethren and sisters here among the Bangoni.[47]

In a sense Koyi's words were prophetic, for, following his return to Malawi in 1881 it was among the Ngoni (albeit the northern, rather than the southern Ngoni) that he was to spend the remaining years of his life, and it is upon his pioneering work there that his missionary reputation rightly rests.

Ngoni Attitudes to the Xhosa Evangelists

In the years from 1882 onwards the work of the Xhosa evangelists William Koyi and George Williams was almost entirely confined to the Ngoni area in what is now the Mzimba district of northern Malawi. There were good reasons for this. The Ngoni had migrated from Natal in the 1820s, and, though the group which finally settled in Malawi around 1855 was extremely heterogeneous, the culture and language of the ruling élite was still essential Nguni, and similar to that of the Xhosa evangelists. It therefore made good sense to use them to work with the Ngoni. In the case of Koyi, at least, the relationship with the Ngoni became very close. In 1883, for example, he wrote to Laws, 'I am quite at home with the Angoni. They have a true love for me; I the same for them'.[48]

For some of the Scottish missionaries notably Elmslie, who arrived amongst the Ngoni early in 1885, this close relationship between the Xhosa evangelists and the Ngoni was seen as a weakness, rather than a strength. For Elmslie, too close contact with Ngoni culture carried with it the danger of a reversion to heathen ways. Koyi's qualities were so obvious that his criticisms of him were always muted—though he did complain that

---

[46] Mapassa Ntintili, various letters in *Christian Express*, 1878-79.

[47] William Koyi to Mapassa Ntintili, quoted from Ntintili to [probably] John Knox Bokwe, 2nd September 1878, in *Christian Express*, December 1878, 9.

[48] William Koyi to Robert Laws, Angoni country, 4th August 1883, Shepperson Collection, NLS.

Mr. Koyi's ability to know the people is invaluable but there is not that weight with him which a white man carries. There is a danger in knowing the people too well and while Koyi is invaluable here there is not that respect shown to him which should be and which is a factor in raising the people from their low condition.[49]

With Williams, Elmslie's relationship was much more negative. He argued that

> Mr. W[illiams] has neither actively nor passively resisted heathen practices, and has given his direct sanction to many of them by attending and taking part in them, e.g. beer drinkings and *ukutomba* [coming of age girls' dances] and marriages within reach. At these latter two many indecencies are engaged in.[50]

In what was a very detailed and complicated dispute, there is no possibility here of apportioning blame, or estimating the accuracy of Elmslie's criticisms. The point is, rather, that Elmslie and Williams represented two very different missiological approaches to African culture—the Scotsman stressing the need to distance oneself from what he perceived as heathen practices; the Xhosa preferring a policy of identification with the people among whom he was working.

But the controversy (which led in the end to Elmslie's threat to resign, and Williams actual resignation) raises another interesting point. How did the Ngoni themselves perceive the Xhosa evangelists? Were they seen primarily as black Europeans, or were they regarded as fellow Africans (and even, perhaps, fellow Ngoni)? One starting point for such an enquiry could be the siNgoni nicknames given to the two Xhosa evangelists. Koyi was known as Mtusane:[51] the bridge-builder, the go-between, or the peace-maker[52]; Williams was given the name Mtandani: a word whose meaning seems to be 'the one who is well-liked', or, 'the trustworthy one', though it is also possible that it indicates 'one who needs the love and affection of others'.[53]

A further linguistic and cultural clue can be gleaned by an exchange between the Ngoni and Elmslie, following Koyi's death in June 1886. Several of the Ngoni councillors asked Elmslie who was to be the *umteteleli* now that Koyi was dead. Elmslie was quite annoyed by the question,

---

[49] Ibid., Elmslie to Laws, 9th June 1885
[50] Elmslie to Laws, Njuyu, 18th September 1888, Livingstonia Papers, National Archives of Malawi.
[51] The Ngoni paramount M'mbelwa gave this name to one of his sons.
[52] See 'A Note on the Names of William Koyi' in this volume.
[53] Kropf and Godfrey, *A Kafir-English Dictionary*, (second edition), Lovedale, 1915, 404; J.L. Döhne, *A Zulu-Kafir Dictionary*, Cape Town, 1857, 338.

assuming that the siNgoni word umteteleli meant simply 'an interpreter' and commented that 'they must have such an one even though I could make them understand but they won't try to do so, being so long accustomed to Mr. Koyi's ways'.[54] The word *umteteleli*, however, had a much deeper meaning than merely an interpreter. It meant an advocate, an intercessor; even one who had the power to judge a case, and therefore to forgive.[55] It was even the word used to translate the Greek word for the Holy Spirit (*parakletos*) in the Xhosa translation of the Bible which William Koyi carried with him when he moved amongst the Ngoni. They, of course, were not equating Koyi with the Holy Spirit: at the time of the discussion there had not been a single baptism amongst the Ngoni. Rather, the point is that the word symbolised for both the Xhosa and the Ngoni, someone of considerable importance, who stood between two parties, who understood both, and who had advocatory authority in relations between them.

Conclusion

In many ways this incident sums up the dilemma of identity for the Xhosa evangelists who worked in Malawi between 1876 and 1888. They were men between two worlds, with a foot in each camp, but never totally at home in either. To the Scottish missionaries amongst whom they worked, they were, in some ways colleagues, but, at the end of the day, most would have agreed with Elmslie's view that they did not have 'that weight...which a white man carries'.[56]

To the Ngoni they were also an enigma. In some ways one of themselves—speaking the same language, understanding the culture, prepared to sit talking for hours in the cattle kraal. And yet, not quite the same: dressing differently, living in different houses, following 'the Book', teaching the white man's ways.

In retrospect, however, it was this very ambiguity which was their strength. William Koyi especially had been brought up as what missionaries of the day in the Eastern Cape liked to call 'a red Kaffir'. He had lived in and knew both the world of traditional African cosmology, and that of the new book-learning which Lovedale instilled. He, and the other Xhosa evangelists, were able to understand and empathise with the people amongst whom they were working in a way which the Scottish missionaries never could. Koyi was not simply Mtusane—a bridge-builder. He, and the other

---

[54] Elmslie to Laws, 5th November 1886, Shepperson Collection.
[55] J.L. Döhne, *A Zulu-Kafir Dictionary*, Cape Town, 1857, 342.
[56] Elmslie to Laws, 9th June 1885, Shepperson Collection.

Xhosa evangelists were, almost literally, bridges. They themselves spanned two worlds, and, in doing so, allowed both missionary and Malawian to pass more easily between one and the other. That in doing so they were sometimes trampled upon by both sides was perhaps an inevitable part of their Christian calling.

Xhosa Missionaries to Malawi: Identity and Photography

Introduction

At the end of May 1876, Dr. James Stewart, principal of the Lovedale Institution in the Eastern Cape region of South Africa, called together his senior pupils, and read to them a letter from the Scottish missionary Dr. Robert Laws. Laws had recently arrived on the shores of Lake Malawi, as part of the pioneer party of the Livingstonia mission of the Free Church of Scotland – sent out to Central Africa in 1875, as a memorial to David Livingstone.

In the letter, Laws described the conditions of the newly established mission, and continued: 'We have a splendid field here for native catechists or men from Lovedale. In a short time we shall be ready for them.' [1]

Stewart had a particular interest in what Laws was writing, for, following Livingstone's funeral in April 1874, it had been he who had first suggested to the Free Church of Scotland that they set up a mission in memory of Livingstone, and that they name it Livingstonia. [2] Though he himself, as principal of Lovedale, was unable to accompany the pioneer party in 1875 to what is now Malawi, he retained a lively interest in the undertaking. Thus, when Laws' letter arrived, he immediately called together the senior male pupils at Lovedale, and asked for volunteers to join the mission in Central Africa.

Photographs in Port Elizabeth

Of the fourteen who initially volunteered, four were chosen to become missionaries to Malawi. They were William Koyi, Shadrach Mngunana, Isaac Williams Wauchope, and Mapassa Ntintili. [3] Within a few weeks of their volunteering, they were on their way to Malawi. To begin with they travelled by train to Port Elizabeth. Here, in July 1876, before boarding ship for East Africa, they went to the studio of A H Board, where they had at least two photographs taken. [4] In addition to the one reproduced here of the four Xhosa

---

[1] *Christian Express*, 1st June 1876, 1.
[2] James Stewart, *Livingstonia: its Origin*, 46-48.
[3] *Lovedale News*, 16th June 1876, 2.
[4] A contemporary print from the original negative still exists as Pic. 1047, in the Lovedale Papers held at the Cory Library for Historical Research, Rhodes University, Grahamstown, South Africa.

missionaries themselves, another was taken of the larger mission party, made up of the four Xhosa and six Europeans.

Lovedale Missionaries

The latter included James Stewart himself, who now felt able to leave Lovedale for a temporary period, while he checked on the progress of the

Livingstonia mission, which he had helped to establish. No contemporary print of this second photograph appears to have survived, though a copy does appear in R H W Shepherd's book *Lovedale, South Africa, 1824-1955*.[5]

Both photographs are typical of their genre – the Victorian African studio photograph. One function of this genre was to try to re-create in the studio – sometimes even in the *European* studio – a feeling for and of Africa. This often included palm fronds, animal skins, rocks, and sometimes even painted scenery. One good example of this genre from the same period is a series of photos taken of Henry Morton Stanley and his young gun-bearer and personal servant Kalulu. In the twelve months after they returned, first to Britain, and then to USA, after Stanley's meeting with Livingstone at Ujiji in November 1871, Stanley had many studio photographs taken of himself and Kalulu.[6] In these photographs, Stanley appears dressed as an African explorer, complete with gun and tropical helmet, while Kalulu appears in a variety of poses, but all aimed at emphasizing his otherness. Sometimes this is done by showing him only in his waistcloth, naked from the waist up. In another version he is carrying an African spear and shield.

Black Europeans or African Christians

In our photograph here of the Xhosa missionaries to Malawi, there is, however, a major paradox. In some ways it is typical of the African studio photograph: there is the tropical vegetation (just visible in the top right-hand corner), the leopard skin, the rustic fencing, and the grass beneath their feet. In other ways, however, the photograph is very untypical, for, far from showing the four Xhosa as exotic others, it presents them in a very European mode: dressed in extremely fashionable clothes, and looking very much like stylish young European gentlemen of the mid-Victorian period. On the simple factual level there is a straightforward explanation for this. Immediately after their selection to go to Malawi, contributions towards an Outfit Fund for the new missionaries were sought from staff and pupils at Lovedale. As a result of the money raised, Koyi, Wauchope, Mngunana and Ntintili were able to buy themselves new outfits for the exciting journey ahead. They appear in both photographs from Board's studio then, dressed, if not in their *Sunday* best, then certainly in their *missionary* best.

---

[5] This much smaller book, published in 1955 should not be confused with Shepherd's centenary history *Lovedale: South Africa 1841-1941*, which contains a very good copy of the photograph of the four Xhosa missionaries, used in this article.
[6] Two such photographs are reproduced in Frank McLynn's *Stanley: the Making of an African Explorer*.

In some respects this may be seen as a composite 'before and after' image of African missions. Such images were popular at the time: indeed one such appears both in an illustrated history of Lovedale itself, and in the autobiography of James Stewart himself, where, on the same page, two contrasting images are titled 'the natives as they are at home' and 'the natives when civilised'.[7] The first image is an African village scene; the second is taken on the lawns of the Lovedale institution itself, with the impressive building in the background, and a group of female pupils in the foreground, dressed in fashionable European clothes. Such 'before and after' photographs were not, of course, confined to African missions. They were also used in Native-American contexts, and in the context of Christian orphanages, such as Dr. Barnardo's. In our present photograph the contrast is implied rather than explicit. What is also implied, of course, is the close connection between religious conversion, and cultural transformation. To become Christian in the late nineteenth century Cape was not simply a statement of religious faith; it meant also to adopt many of the trappings of European civilisation - not least the European sartorial fashions of the day.

This cultural transformation was undoubtedly something at which the Scottish missionaries were aiming; but it was also enthusiastically embraced by most of the Xhosa pupils themselves at Lovedale. This may be seen in many of the photographs taken at Lovedale during this period, when both men and women were not simply dressed in European fashions, but elegantly and fashionably dressed.[8] It may be sensed also in the pages of the *Christian Express* - the newspaper produced monthly by Lovedale (though admittedly largely controlled by the missionaries themselves at this period). Here are reports of the Literary and Debating Society, the Independent Order of True Templars (the 'native' version of the International Order of Good Templars - a leading temperance movement of the day), the Lovedale cricket team, and so on. That Leon de Kock has titled a recent book on education at Lovedale, *Civilising Barbarians*[9] is startling enough; what is even more startling is that the title is based on a phrase from a letter, written, not by the Scottish missionaries, but by a group of leading Lovedale pupils them-

---

[7] James Wells, *Stewart of Lovedale*, opposite p. 364.
[8] Many of these photographs may be found in the Lovedale Papers of the Cory Library for Historical Research, Rhodes University, Grahamstown. Several of them have been published in such books as Shepherd's *Lovedale, South Africa: 1841-1941,* and Stewart's *Lovedale, South Africa: Illustrated by Fifty Views from Photographs.*
[9] Leon de Kock, *Civilising Barbarians: Missionary Narrative and African Textual Response in Nineteenth Century South Africa.*

selves[10] - including Isaac Wauchope, one of the four missionaries to go to Malawi, and including the signatures of several others who had volunteered for Livingstonia in 1876.

Yet it would be wrong to accept this stereotype simply at its face value, and to assume that the products of Lovedale in the 1870s were abandoning their African culture in favour of a European version. Rather, in postcolonial terms our photograph represents the *hybridity* of educated Christian Xhosa identity in the 1870s. We must be careful, on the other hand, not to imply that the European culture, seemingly being adopted so enthusiastically, was simply a superficial surface gloss, covering the old African 'heathen' and 'savage' reality. This was the argument of many of those racially motivated opponents of missionary education in Africa – especially of the higher education which an institution such as Lovedale offered. Rather, the reality was that the Xhosa converts of Lovedale had genuinely adopted certain aspects of the European tradition, while, at the same time, retaining many of the deeply held values of their own African culture. Though we do not have time to deal with them here, these values may be seen regularly contesting the dominant discourse of Scottish missionary assumptions, in the black press and the Xhosa literature of the period. One good example of this is the periodical *Imvo Zabantsundu*[11] edited by John Tengo Jabavu (himself a graduate of Lovedale). The bi-lingual production (in both Xhosa and English) itself illustrates the hybrid nature of the new black educated élite; but this should not blind us to the fact that the periodical is often at the forefront of debate over what we may here call African issues. We can see similar African concerns and priorities in contemporary Xhosa literature - both oral and written, for example, in the poetry of people such as Isaac Wauchope, [12] after his return from Malawi, and the music of John Knox Bokwe, another of the fourteen original volunteers for Livingstonia in 1876.

---

[10] *Civilising Barbarians*, 97-99.

[11] *Imvo Zabantsundu* (meaning 'Black Opinion' or 'the Views of the Black People') was founded by John Tengo Jabavu in 1884. Jabavu had previously been editor of *Isigidimi sama Xosa*, a Lovedale publication, but wanted more editorial freedom than the mission periodical allowed him.

[12] Among the most famous of Wauchope's poems was *Yilwani ngosiba (Fight with the Pen)* which uses African idiom to urge the Xhosa to fight for their rights by education, rather than in battle. Similar views are expressed in his poem *Imbumba yama Nyama (*an idiomatic Xhosa phrase very difficult to translate literally, but which here might be rendered *Complete Unity*). Wauchope was a leading founder of one of the earliest black political organisations in the Cape, also called Imbumba yama Nyama, which was founded in 1882.

The Xhosa Missionaries in Malawi

The paradox and tension which is inherent in the photograph of the four Xhosa missionaries to Malawi may be seen also in their missionary careers in Malawi. Before looking at a few aspects of this paradox, let us survey very briefly the four men and their subsequent careers. Possibly the most academically able of the four was Shadrach Mngunana, who was sent to Malawi as a teacher. He began teaching in the school at Cape Maclear, at the south end of Lake Malawi, where the Livingstonia mission had established its base when it first arrived in 1875. Early missionary reports of his work were very encouraging. [13] Within nine months, however, he was dead: an early victim of fever, and a blow to the European hope that black Africans would be better able to withstand the rigours of a Central African climate than would the Scots. Isaac Williams Wauchope lasted an even shorter time, though his illness was not fatal. Before he even reached Lake Malawi, he was victim of recurrent bouts of fever, which led to hallucinations and occasional violent outbursts. Stewart decided to send him back to South Africa; and though his missionary career in Malawi was over almost before it had begun, he recovered, and went on to make important contributions in several fields, as Xhosa poet, local historian, Christian minister, temperance activist, and campaigner for African higher education.[14] Mapassa Ntintili, a wagon-maker by trade, spent almost four years in Malawi, before returning to the Eastern Cape, where he became a teacher and an evangelist - eventually dying in 1897.[15] During his time in Malawi he had worked, not only at the Free Church of Scotland Livingstonia mission at Cape Maclear, but also at the Blantyre mission of the Church of Scotland - playing an important part in its survival at a critical time in its early history.

In Malawi, by far the best remembered of the four was William Koyi: the only one of the group to return for a second period of service after his leave in South Africa in 1880-81. During his first period of service from 1876-1880, Koyi had established a reputation as an indispensable part of the mission. He was particularly useful as an interpreter: especially when the mission made contact with the Ngoni people (who had migrated from the KwaZulu region of South Africa in the 1820s. Their language was similar to

---

[13] Dr. Black to Dr. Smith, Livingstonia, 3rd March 1877, Livingstonia Papers, National Library of Scotland.

[14] For details of Wauchope's later career see, T. Jack Thompson, *Touching the Heart: Xhosa Missionaries to Malawi, 1876-88*, chapter 8, 'Redeeming Failure: a postscript on Isaac Wauchope'.

[15] An obituary appeared in the Livingstonia mission periodical *Aurora*, Vol. 2, 1898.

Koyi's own Xhosa tongue. Both before and after his return, William Koyi worked as a pioneer missionary among the Ngoni - especially the northern Ngoni of paramount chief M'mbelwa. He died among the Ngoni in 1886, and his grave is still marked and revered to-day - more than 110 years later.[16]

Hybridity and Identity

To conclude, I want to look briefly at a few examples of the hybridity[17] of Xhosa Christian identity, as seen in the career of the Xhosa missionaries to Malawi. The first point to make is that they were almost never called 'missionaries' at the time. They were almost always referred to as 'evangelists' or 'volunteers', and were seen as fulfilling a role clearly inferior to that of the Scots. Yet the Scots missionaries expected them to behave like black Europeans, rather than like African Christians. One very small example of this was an early criticism made by Stewart of Isaac Wauchope, on the journey up to Lake Malawi. In his youthful enthusiasm (he and Mngunana were both in their mid-twenties when they set out for Malawi) Wauchope wanted to be of as much help as possible. When the boat in which they were travelling up the Shire River frequently ran aground on rocks, Wauchope was one of the first to jump into the water to try to push it off again. But rather than praising him for his enthusiasm and hard work, Stewart criticised him for 'working in the boats like a raw native'.[18] On the other hand, once the Xhosa missionaries were settled in Malawi, they themselves began to complain that they were being forced to do too much manual work, and were not given enough opportunity for evangelistic outreach. That there was substance in their complaints seems to be indicated by the fact that in July 1880 the Livingstonia committee in Glasgow ruled that 'the evangelists should not work more than three days a week at manual exercise'.[19]

In later years, the Scottish missionary Angus Elmslie was to criticise both William Koyi (and a fifth, later Xhosa missionary, George Williams) for getting too close to the Ngoni. He wrote: 'There is a danger in knowing the

---

[16] In June 1996, a memorial service was held at the grave, at which M'mbelwa IV, paramount chief of the northern Ngoni, was present.

[17] The word hybridity has been popularised in postcolonial studies by (amongst others) Homi Bhabha. It refers to the mixture of ethnicity, language, religion and culture with which colonised peoples have to cope, and is, I believe, particularly applicable to the Xhosa missionaries to Malawi.

[18] James Stewart to Alexander Duff, 4th December 1876, Ms. 7876, Livingstonia Papers, National Library of Scotland.

[19] Minutes of the Livingstonia sub-committee, 22nd July 1880, Ms. 7912, Livingstonia Papers, National Library of Scotland.

people too well, and while Koyi is invaluable here, there is not that respect shown to him which should be, and which is a factor in raising the people from their low condition.'[20] Elmslie's ideal for the Xhosa missionaries was perhaps what appears on the surface of the photograph taken by A H Board in July 1876: a group of four black Europeans, indistinguishable, except by skin colour, from their Scottish colleagues. But the last known photograph of William Koyi taken in Malawi is a more accurate reflection, both of the cultural reality, and of the missiological importance of the Xhosa missionaries.

Koy, Laws and the Ngoni

It shows a group of Ngoni warriors, led by Chiputula Nhlane, making what is probably their first visit to the newly opened mission station of Bandawe on the shores of Lake Malawi. Seated amongst them are the Scottish missionary Robert Laws, and William Koyi.[21] Laws looks nervous and ill at ease - perhaps due to his awareness of the Ngoni reputation as fearsome warriors. Koyi, dressed in a loosely fitting jacket seems to merge with the Ngoni. Only a knowledge of Koyi's features, or a close examination of the photograph would serve to distinguish him from his fellow Africans. It is not simply that his elegant new clothes, bought just before Board's portrait in

---

[20] Elmslie to Laws, 9th June 1885, Shepperson Collection, University of Edinburgh.

[21] A copy of this photograph appears in W. P. Livingstone, *Laws of Livingstonia*, opposite p. 113, and also in Jack Thompson, *Touching the Heart*, 110.

July 1876, have grown old and shabby; it is rather that Koyi has begun to find his vocation: identification with the Ngoni amongst whom he lived and worked. It was in this identification that the real missionary significance of the Xhosa missionaries lay, rather than in the gentrified poses of Board's studio photograph. And yet Board's photograph is not totally misleading either, for, in its own way, it shows a group of young men caught between two worlds, and struggling to find a new identity which retains the best of both. In that sense, at least, this photograph of the Xhosa missionaries to Malawi, taken one hundred and thirty years ago, remains relevant in the early years of this new century of African Christianity.

William Koyi and the Ngoni

Introduction

We are here today[1] to celebrate the opening of Njuyu station just over 120 years ago. In particular, in this lecture I want to concentrate on the work of William Koyi.

Together with his Xhosa colleagues, Isaac Williams Wauchope, Shadrach Mngunana and Mapassa Ntintili, William Koyi had first come to Malawi with the second Livingstonia party in 1876. Later he was joined by a fifth Xhosa missionary, George Williams, who also worked among the Ngoni between 1884 and 1888; but of all these black South Africans who worked in Malawi in the 1870s and 1880s, William Koyi was undoubtedly the most important. Koyi was a Xhosa, born in the Eastern Cape around 1846. He became a student at Lovedale, the great Scottish missionary institution, in 1870. In 1876, he was one of those who volunteered to come to Malawi to help the Livingstonia mission.

At first Koyi worked at Cape Maclear, and even helped out in the early days of the Blantyre mission. In 1878 he came to Kaning'ina, near Mzuzu. The station at Kaning'ina, on the edge of Ngoni territory, remained open for less than a year, and closed in October 1879. William Koyi would have been keen to stay there, but Robert Laws thought it was too far removed from the main station at Bandawe, too isolated and difficult to supply with food. So the station was closed. No trace of it remains today. William Koyi returned to Bandawe, and worked there for a few more months before he returned to South Africa on leave in 1880.

The Beginning of Work at Njuyu

Just before Christmas 1881, William Koyi arrived back at Bandawe[2], for his second, and, as it was to turn out, his last tour of duty with the Livingstonia mission. It was well over a year and a half since he had left Malawi, and there must have been times when, in spite of his personal eagerness to return, he had wondered whether he would ever get back. The disputes between Stewart, Laws, and the Livingstonia committee over the site of a new (and hopefully more healthy) headquarters, as well as the terms of service, and

---

[1] A shorter version of this lecture was first given at the celebrations at Njuyu on 18th April 2004 to commemorate the beginning of Scottish missionary work among the northern Ngoni.
[2] Robert Laws' diary, 22 December 1881, Laws' papers, EUL.

salaries of the Lovedale evangelists, had grossly extended what was meant to have been a comparatively short period of leave. One practical outcome of the unduly long stay was that Koyi's colleague Mapassa Ntintili—no doubt disillusioned by the protracted disputes about his and Koyi's return, and possibly not entirely ignorant of Robert Laws reluctance to have him back—had taken a job as a teacher in the Transkei, and was never to return to Malawi.

During his time back in the Eastern Cape, William Koyi had married the second daughter of Rev. Andries van Rooyen.[3] The van Rooyen family was well known in the Fort Beaufort/Alice area. The father, Andries had been ordained as a Congregationalist minister in 1849—earlier even than the more famous Tiyo Soga (who, in any case, had been ordained as a Presbyterian minister in Scotland, before returning to the Cape)—and served as minister of the Blinkwater congregation until his death in March 1880.[4] He and his wife had four children—two sons and two daughters. Of the daughters very little is recorded: (I have been unable to find even their names.) The sons, James and Timothy, by contrast, were well-known figures in the Lovedale of the early and mid-1870s, and were acquaintances, and perhaps even friends, of William Koyi. Like Koyi (and most of the rest of the Livingstonia volunteers) they were members of the Independent Order of True Templars.[5] Koyi arrived back at Lovedale just after the death of their father. It is not clear how well, if at all, he had known Miss van Rooyen before going to Livingstonia. She does not appear in any of the Lovedale class-lists of the period, and it is likely that she may have attended instead the Methodist school at Healdstown. However well he knew her, Miss van Rooyen was not William Koyi's first love.

William Koyi and Tause Soga

While studying at Lovedale, Koyi had fallen in love with a young woman who had arrived there at much the same time as he had himself. She was Tause[6] Soga (a niece of Tiyo Soga, and daughter of his brother Zaze).[7] The attraction seems to have been mutual, but Tause's father disapproved of the

---

[3] *Lovedale Past and Present,* 'William Koyi', 126.

[4] *Christian Express*, April 1880, 2.

[5] *Lovedale News*, 1(1), May 1876, 2.

[6] Tause's name is spelt both *Tause* and *Tausi* in various places. It is even possible that *Tawuse* might be a better rendering. However, I have used *Tause*, which was the commonest form in the 1870s.

[7] In his monumental book *Frontiers*, Noel Mostert confuses this Tause Soga with her aunt of the same name. (See caption to illustration of Tause Soga in *Frontiers*, after page 896).

match[8]—probably because Koyi was from a very much humbler background than the Sogas. Tause was packed off to Scotland to continue her education, in the company of her friend Martha Kwatsha, who was later to marry Mpambani Mzimba. The later register of Lovedale pupils *Lovedale Past and Present* put it rather more discreetly, 'In January 1874 her friends deemed it advisable to send her to Scotland.'[9] There she studied at the Free Church normal seminary in Glasgow, though she seems also to have spent at least some of the time as a pupil of Dollar Academy in Clackmannan, where a member of the Soga family, Dr. Hector Soga, still teaches.[10]

A portrait of Tause, taken at this time in Glasgow,[11] shows her as a beautiful, dignified, but sad young woman. It seems that the affection between her and Koyi did not end with her departure for Scotland. Jane Waterston (who had been her headmistress at Lovedale) was herself in Britain while Tause Soga and Martha Kwatsha were studying in Scotland. Writing to James Stewart from London in May 1876, she commented: 'Even being at home [by which Jane Waterston meant Britain] has not driven [Koyi] out of Tause Soga's head for it was her father refused him, not she.'[12] No such information about William Koyi's continuing emotions on the matter is available; but it is at least interesting to speculate whether his decision to volunteer for Livingstonia in May 1876, might not have been connected in some way with his frustration at Tause's absence in Scotland, and the probability that her family would prohibit any continuing relationship between them after her return.

Tause Soga and Martha Kwatsha left England on the return voyage to South Africa in September 1876, at precisely the same time that Koyi and the Lovedale party were on the last stages of their journey between the Cape and lake Malawi. The two women might well have gone on board ship to return to South Africa with very different emotions, for while (if Jane Waterston is to be believed) Tause was still in love with William Koyi, her friend Martha was going home to be married to Mpambani Mzimba, who, a few months earlier, had become the first black Presbyterian minister to be ordained in South Africa. Whatever their emotions, they were brutally interrupted as their ship, *the Windsor Castle* approached Cape Town. On 19th

---

[8] *Letters of Jane Elizabeth Waterston*, Jane Waterston to James Stewart, 14 May 1876.

[9] *Lovedale Past and Present*, 491-2.

[10] Personal communication with Dr. Hector Soga.

[11] The portrait was taken at the Glasgow studio of Thomas Annan, who had taken photos of David Livingstone in 1857—one of which was used to create the etching which made up the frontispiece of Livingstone's *Last Journals*.

[12] *Letters of Jane Waterston,* 109.

October, within sight of its destination, *the Windsor Castle* ran aground off Dassen Island.[13] Though all of the passengers were rescued, the experience must have been both mentally and physically traumatic. While Tause went on to be bridesmaid at the wedding of Martha Kwatsha and Mpambani Mzimba,[14] she never really recovered from the experience off Dassen Island, and soon fell ill with tuberculosis. *Lovedale Past and Present* speculated that the disease was brought on by the combination of 'the shock, added to the effects of her residence in a cold damp climate like that of Scotland.'[15] Whatever the cause, her condition steadily deteriorated, and she died on 22nd March 1877.[16]

No record remains of how William Koyi heard of her death, or his reaction to the news. It is likely that news of it would have reached him at much the same time that his friend and colleague Shadrach Mngunana was dying at Cape Maclear. By the time he was preparing to return from Malawi to the Cape nearly three years later, he had decided to marry, with the expectation that he would soon be back, working in Malawi. The long delay before his return emphasises the uncertain future of the whole Lovedale undertaking to Malawi. For all the important work he had done during his first period in Malawi, if William Koyi had not returned in 1881, he would have been no more than a tiny footnote in the history of Christianity there . By contrast, his eventual return, and his final years' work as a missionary among the Ngoni in what is now Mzimba district, have established him as one of the most significant figures in the early spread of Christianity in Malawi.

The Move to uNgoni

In spite of his recent marriage, Koyi returned alone to Malawi. There seem to have been two reasons for this. The first was that the likelihood of Koyi going to open a new station among the Ngoni made the presence of his new wife somewhat problematical in terms of personal safety. The new work was likely to be dangerous and very demanding physically, and Mrs. Koyi had no previous experience of living in such isolated conditions. The second was that she does not seem to have been in very robust health at the time. As a result, a decision was taken to delay her departure north, and, as it turned out, it was to be November 1884 before she finally arrived among the Ngoni.

---

[13] *Lovedale News*, 25 October 1876, 3-4.
[14] Brock, 'James Stewart', 348.
[15] *Lovedale Past and Present*, 492.
[16] *Ibid.*

The lack of any missionary who could communicate fluently with the Ngoni during Koyi's extended absence at the Cape, meant that contact with them during this period had been limited. This, in its turn, had created suspicion among the Ngoni that the mission was abandoning them in favour of an alliance with the lakeshore Tonga. Such a conclusion must have been strengthened as Koyi's promised return was repeatedly delayed, and as, following the transfer of the mission headquarters to Bandawe in 1881, new buildings began to be erected there. For these reasons, and also because the instructions of the Livingstonia committee had included the opening of a station among the Ngoni, Laws was keen to resume work there as soon as practicable after the return of Koyi. The onset of the wet season would not have made this very easy, but, nevertheless, Koyi went up to uNgoni, to visit M'mbelwa in January 1882, shortly after his arrival back in northern Malawi.[17] In April 1882, Laws and the recently arrived missionary Hannington set out for uNgoni to make contact with Ngoni leaders, and formally establish the first permanent station among the Ngoni.[18] By the time they arrived, considerable ground-work for the opening of Njuyu station had already been done by Koyi.

The most productive early contacts with the Ngoni had been with the Nhlane clan, and it was near Chiputula Nhlane's village of Hoho, at the foot of Njuyu mountain, on the eastern bank of the Kasitu river, that the missionaries decided to build their first station. Echigodhlweni the village of chief M'mbelwa, was situated a couple of kilometres away, to the west of the river. Subsequent images of mission stations tend to make us see such places as substantial settlements made up of several sturdy brick buildings linked by roads. The reality was that, to begin with, and for some considerable time afterwards, Njuyu was made up of temporary mud and wattle huts—a fact that seemed to trouble William Koyi more than it did Robert Laws, as we shall see later.

Though the Ngoni were jealous of the presence of the mission among the Tonga, this did not mean that the establishment of an Ngoni mission settlement was a straightforward matter. For the next few years there were competing factions among the Ngoni—some wanting to welcome the mission for the supposed political and economic advantage which its presence might bring, others much less positive about the prospect. In addition, there was a

---

[17] Koyi to Laws, 23 January 1882, Shepperson Collection, Special Collections, Edinburgh University Library.

[18] Laws' Diary, 18 April 1882, Special Collections, Edinburgh University Library.

good deal of rivalry about where any possible mission station might be placed.

Laws was the first to admit that Koyi's part in negotiating a peaceful resolution of these tensions was central. He wrote:

> In all these negotiations Mr. Wm. Koyi has been my right hand. Not only has he acted as my interpreter, and an interpreter whose heart was thoroughly in what was being said, but he has been my trusty adviser in what might best be left unsaid, as well as the manner of putting what I did say. The advantage of having a Christian native, acquainted with the prejudices and mode of thought of the natives cannot be over-estimated.[19]

Laws was a man not easily given to extravagant praise, so the passage which immediately followed that quoted above was all the more surprising, and perhaps represents his most generous assessment of the work of the Lovedale missionaries in general, and William Koyi in particular. It is therefore worth quoting at length:

> Again, with regard to Mr. Koyi's work, and that of native evangelists generally, one part requires special mention, because very readily overlooked. In the evenings, or during the day at other villages, Mr. Koyi would go and have long talks, say with one of Chipatula's brothers, or perhaps with a few neighbours, and these conversations turning on spiritual topics or on the conditions of civilized life, an amount of instruction is imparted and friendly feeling cultivated, which the more formal public meetings could never effect. Again, William, as a native, can reach their hearts by like habits of thought and speech, in a way which I suspect no European, however great an adept at the language, could ever hope to reach. In the white skin there is something at once alien, which, though it may draw attention, and, to some extent, respect, does not touch the heart as William's presence does.[20]

As we shall see below, such a positive view of the work of William Koyi in particular, and the Lovedale evangelists in general was to be in stark contrast to the views of Angus Elmslie, soon to arrive as a missionary doctor among the Ngoni.

The same issue of the *Christian Express* in which Laws' comments appeared, also published a long composite letter from William Koyi himself, which was an amalgam of various letters in Xhosa and English which he had sent back to Lovedale. Obviously written in 1882, these letters paint an optimistic picture of work amongst the Ngoni.[21] Koyi records that he preaches each Sunday at Chipatula's village, and sometimes has a congregation of between one and two hundred. He speaks of waiting for the

---

[19] Letter of Robert Laws, 12 June 1882, quoted in *Christian Express*, April 1883, 54-56.
[20] *Ibid.*
[21] *Ibid.*, 49-50.

permission of M'mbelwa before opening schools, but does not anticipate any trouble. A school was, in fact, briefly opened, but it seems that Chiputula was alerted that M'mbelwa was not in favour of it, and forced Koyi to close it again until the chief's permission was obtained. In fact, this turned out to be one of the most contentious questions of the next few years, and it was not until shortly before Koyi's death in June 1886 that permission was finally granted.

The reasons for M'mbelwa's reluctance to allow education were complicated. On the one hand he had a somewhat superstitious understanding of what education entailed, and, believing it to convey some sort of mystical power, was reluctant to allow children to receive it before he himself was initiated. On a more pragmatic level many of the older Ngoni *indunas* realised that their people stood at a turning point in their history, a quarter of a century after settling in northern Malawi, following their thirty year migration from South Africa. Their capacity successfully to continue with a way of life based on raiding and military prowess was now being challenged by the increasingly effective defensive techniques of groups such as the Tonga, and by the spread of guns among those the Ngoni might have attacked. The successful spread of missionary education would clearly further undermine the traditional way of life of the Ngoni, by providing the next generation of potential warriors with an alternative lifestyle.

The edgy situation which the question of permission to open schools represented, was, in fact symptomatic of a much wider unease between the mission and sections of the Ngoni, which was to continue for several years, up to, and beyond William Koyi's death. While paramount chief M'mbelwa himself remained reasonably friendly throughout—especially with Robert Laws and William Koyi—some of the other chiefs, such as Mtwalo, and many of the *indunas*[22] were much more ambivalent about the mission. It was precisely in this situation that the steady conscientious work of William Koyi was so valuable during these years.

The Work of Koyi amongst the Ngoni

Of particular significance in these early stages was Koyi's sensitivity to Ngoni fears and uncertainties, and his interpretation of these to Laws at Bandawe. Central to this was the question (from the Ngoni perspective) of what the missionary intentions were in their territory, and whether (unlike their last stay at Kaning'ina, which lasted less than a year) they intended to settle permanently in uNgoni. Complicating the matter further, as indicated above,

---

[22] *Induna* may be translated as councillor or advisor.

was the fact that while some Ngoni welcomed the missionary presence—especially if it meant what they saw as an alliance against the Tonga—others were much less positive about it, and the insidious effects it might have on traditional Ngoni culture.

In January 1882, William Koyi, accompanied by Albert Namalambe, the first convert of the mission at Cape Maclear, and recently baptised at Bandawe, and the usual posse of carriers, had arrived in uNgoni. Initially they visited Chiputula Nhlane, and then M'mbelwa. Following permission to settle at Hoho, 'William Koyi took possession of Ngoniland for Christ'[23] as Elmslie was somewhat grandiosely to put it several years later. Koyi's own description was characteristically much more humble: 'I feel myself very small for this work of laying a foundation for so great a work'.[24] While Namalambe returned to Bandawe, with letters from Koyi to Laws, setting out the situation in uNgoni, Koyi himself began the process of establishing a permanent mission presence at Njuyu. In April, Laws and Hannington (together with Koyi) visited M'mbelwa to confirm the missionary intention to settle in the area. During the next few months, a succession of Scottish colleagues came and went at Njuyu. Initially, Hannington took seriously ill with fever, and Laws called both Hannington's and his own wife up to Njuyu, as it was thought possible that Hannington would not recover.[25] He eventually did, and was able to proceed back to Scotland on sick leave. In July, Koyi was joined by the artisan James Sutherland, and they began the process of putting up more sturdy buildings—though they were as yet wattle and daub, rather than brick. In November the teacher John Smith joined Koyi briefly, and in January 1883, Peter McCallum settled at Njuyu.[26]

These years were extremely tense ones for the mission, as various factions in the Ngoni vied for supremacy. In particular, the question of Ngoni grievances against the Tonga on the lakeshore, and uncertainty about where the missionaries stood in the dispute, made it a time of great strain for Koyi and his colleagues. Koyi was particularly aware of the need to keep the Ngoni informed of what the missionaries were doing, and to reassure them that the missionary presence was permanent and benevolent among them. One indication of this, he thought, would be the construction of more per-

---

[23] Elmslie, *Among the Wild Ngoni*, 103.
[24] Koyi to Laws, 6 February 1883, Shepperson collection, EUL.
[25] *Laws of Livingstonia*, 199.
[26] Smith to Laws, 28 November 1882, and McCallum to Laws, 20 January 1883, Livingstonia Papers, Acc. 9220, NLS.

manent brick buildings at Njuyu. As early as April 1883 he expressed these views in a letter to Laws at Bandawe:

> I think myself we should make a small breke [*sic*] building. I look at this also that it may be something to show the people that we mean settling among them though they do not quite believe that we came to stay with them…We must get Roots in their country.[27]

As a postscript to the same letter, Koyi informed Laws that he had already made ten thousand bricks, and, in the next few months, he employed up to forty people in brick-making, prior to the construction of a permanent brick house at Njuyu. The house was completed in November 1883. The missionaries named the station *Sibehleli*, which Sutherland translated as 'they are settled'.[28] This, in fact was a slight mistranslation, since the word actually means 'we are settled'. Sutherland's linguistic mistake is a very clear indication that the name had been chosen by William Koyi himself rather than any of his Scottish colleagues. The significance of the name should not be underestimated, indicating, as it does, Koyi's deep concern to establish a more permanent relationship with the Ngoni. Yet the equivalent Ngoni name for the station, shows clearly that this desire was not universally shared on the Ngoni side. One of their nick-names for the mission station at this time was *Ekusinda Nyeriweni*. That this name was well known to the missionaries is indicated by the fact that several of them used or commented on it. Sutherland used it (though in a misspelled form) simply as the address of the station.[29] Elmslie mentions the name in his *Among the Wild Ngoni*, but comments merely that it is 'a term which cannot be translated in polite language'[30]; Charles Stuart, a later missionary to uNgoni, writing many years later, translated it as 'dung-hill'.[31] The literal meaning of the expression seems to be even more derogatory, meaning something like, 'the place where shit is spread around'.[32]

In spite of this Ngoni ambivalence about the presence of the mission, Koyi's steady and patient work, allied to his linguistic and cultural affinity to the Ngoni, began to pay dividends. Though the permission to open a school was quickly withdrawn, Koyi was able to write to Laws in January 1883 that 'at last Mombera has given me freedom to preach in his place and his coun-

---

[27] Koyi to Laws, 5 April 1883, Shepperson collection, EUL.
[28] Sutherland to Laws, 27 November 1883, Livingstonia papers, ACC.9220, NLS.
[29] Sutherland to Laws, 29 September 1883, Livingstonia papers, Acc. 9220, NLS.
[30] *Among the Wild Ngoni*, 158.
[31] Charles Stuart, in an article in the *Free Church of Scotland Monthly* (date unknown).
[32] Doke and Vilakazi, Zulu-English Dictionary, 624 & 757.

try after all'.[33] He wrote also of Chiputula ordering work to stop in his village on a Sunday because 'the white man told him that it is God's day'.[34] The missionaries may have seen this as the beginnings of a small crack in the edifice of Ngoni culture and religion, but in fact, a much more complex dynamic was taking place.

Koyi and Ngoni Culture

In the same letter to Laws, Koyi also mentioned a request from M'mbelwa that he should come to his village and pray for the success of the crops for the coming year. Koyi goes on to describe the service which he led there on the last Sunday of December 1882.[35] He reports that one and a half thousand people turned up at the service to pray for a successful planting season, and while we may have to take his statistics with a pinch of salt, clearly something quite significant was taking place. Obviously it was not a mass conversion to Christianity—the first Ngoni baptisms were still more than seven years in the future. The real significance of the event may lie in its timing. Before leaving South Africa, the Ngoni had regularly followed the traditional ritual of the *incwala*. I have described this ritual in more detail elsewhere.[36] Suffice it to say here that it was a traditional first-fruits ritual among several Nguni groups in southern Africa, and was concerned both with agricultural fertility, and with the annual renewal of the spiritual power of the king. In the southern African context from which the Ngoni had migrated in the 1820s, the ritual took place at the end of December—the precise time that M'mbelwa asked Koyi to come and pray for the crops. As a result of several factors—the long migration, the changing composition of the Ngoni group itself, as it assimilated new non-Zansi[37] elements, the changes in the timing of the agricultural year as the Ngoni moved more than one thousand five hundred miles to the north—the *incwala* had died out amongst the Ngoni by the time that Koyi settled at Njuyu. Nevertheless, it seems reasonable to assume that, particularly amongst the Zansi-Ngoni themselves a clear memory of, and perhaps even a feeling of need for the *incwala* (or at least something which fulfilled a similar function) remained. If this were the case, what the Ngoni were actually doing in asking Koyi to

[33] Koyi to Laws, 19 January 1883, Shepperson collection, EUL.
[34] Ibid.
[35] Ibid.
[36] Thompson, *Christianity in Northern Malawi*, 88-95.
[37] The Ngoni used the term *abaZansi*, meaning 'those from the south', to indicate the original core who had begun the migration from South Africa around 1820.

pray for the crops, was using him as a religious practitioner to fulfill their own traditional religious needs, rather than, in any real sense, agreeing to adopt the new religious allegiance being offered by the missionaries.

Yet there is another point of importance here. This is the willingness of the Xhosa evangelists—both William Koyi, and, later George Williams—to carry out what we might call liminal[38] activities. These may be contrasted with the reluctance of some of the Scottish missionaries (especially Elmslie) to get involved in areas which bordered on traditional religion—or, as they would have regarded it, 'heathen superstition'. Precisely because of their cultural affinity to the Ngoni, both Koyi and later Williams were able to appreciate the importance of such ritual, and were happy to accommodate it within a basically Christian framework.

During 1882 and 1883 Koyi's importance in the work of the mission can hardly be over-estimated. For most, if not all of this period, he was the only missionary who could communicate directly and fluently with the Ngoni. At a period when the Ngoni themselves were going through great uncertainty in their own cultural adjustments to a more settled lifestyle, after more than half a century of migration and raiding, Koyi's sympathetic understanding of their plight, and patient explanation of the mission's position, almost certainly helped to avoid bloodshed and violence on more than one occasion.

At the same time, he acted as what in modern parlance might be termed a consultant to the Scottish missionaries—constantly giving them advice about how to react to the Ngoni. A considerable number of Koyi's letters from this period have survived, as well as letters from other missionaries about him. If one looks, for example, at the letters written by James Sutherland to Robert Laws in the latter part of 1882 as well as some of those of Peter McCallum in 1883 one is struck by the number of times phrases such as 'Mr. Koyi thinks it is better...', 'William thinks', 'William was also thinking' occur.[39] Quite clearly, whatever the social conventions of the day, Koyi was the missionary best placed to know which actions would be most effective in a particular context, and was regarded by the other artisans as effectively in charge of the work.

In the same way, if one looks at Koyi's own letters from the period, one sees him constantly offering advice to Laws about a whole range of cultural

---

[38] By liminal is meant here, activities which were on the borders between Ngoni and missionary culture, and, in particular, activities which might be regarded with suspicion by one or the other culture.

[39] See, for example, Sutherland to Laws, 2 October 1882 and McCallum to Laws, 5 April 1883, Acc.9220, NLS.

and political issues. In the very first letter that he wrote to Laws, after going to Njuyu in January 1882, he was already giving him information and advice about Ngoni-Tonga relations[40]—a subject which was to dominate correspondence for the next few years. On several occasions, Koyi's inside knowledge about what the Ngoni were thinking and planning with regard to the Tonga proved useful to Laws at Bandawe. In these early letters of Koyi's there is no trace of subservience. They are written in an open and straightforward style, and are not afraid to tell Laws where he is going wrong, or, when necessary, to disagree with him. For those familiar with the history of Malawi (and particularly with its photographic representations) the image of Robert Laws which is indelibly fixed on the mind is that of the white-bearded patriarch of the 1910s and 1920s. It is sometimes easy to forget that when Laws first went to Malawi in 1875 he was a young, inexperienced man of twenty-five, and was actually four years younger than William Koyi. While the social and racial conventions of the time clearly placed Laws (as leader of the mission) in a hierarchical position well above Koyi, it is nevertheless the case that in the early 1880s Koyi was willing to give straightforward advice, and the young Robert Laws to accept it. One interesting example of the relationship occurred in December 1882, when Koyi seems to have been alone at Njuyu. Laws wrote to him inviting him to come down to Bandawe for a break over the Christmas and New Year period. It must have been a tempting offer, for as a letter from Koyi made clear a few months later, while he got on well with the Ngoni, he could also feel lonely and isolated. As he said in April 1883, 'I feel it very much to be all alone with no one to speak to… I have the Angoni to speak to, but sometimes very little of things that are of any importance.'[41] So when Laws invited him down to Bandawe he must have been tempted to go. Nevertheless, he replied:

> I would have come down this time as you wish me to do so, but there is this, that storys *(sic)* may go about that we are leaving the country again. So that I think it is better for me to stay until another one comes.[42]

Another such incident occurred early in 1884. At this time, Laws was at home in Scotland, and Bandawe was under the temporary control of Dr. Scott. This time Koyi was not alone at Njuyu. In fact, there were two other missionaries with him—the Scottish artisan Sutherland, and the Xhosa evangelist George Williams, who had recently arrived in uNgoni. On this occasion Koyi's refusal of the invitation was based on the delicate political

---

[40] Koyi to Laws, 23 January 1882, Shepperson collection, EUL.
[41] Ibid., April 1883.
[42] Ibid., 10 December 1882.

situation, and on the fact that he was reluctant to leave his colleagues. He wrote to Laws, 'I could not at the time leave Mr. Sutherland and Williams, as there was a talk Mtwaro and Mperembe was going to [leave] Mambera and go to the other side of the Lake.'[43]

In these two incidents we see clearly Koyi's on-going concern for the effect of missionary actions on the Ngoni. In the first, especially, Koyi is clearly aware that, at this time, and for some considerable period later, the Ngoni were neurotic that the mission was going to abandon them in favour of the Tonga. That Koyi's fears were not groundless is shown by the fact that, in the period immediately following his departure from uNgoni in August 1884 to go and meet his wife who had finally come up from South Africa, the Ngoni were reported to be in a very restless mood, and to believe that Koyi had left them permanently.[44]

The fluctuating Ngoni views on the permanence or otherwise of the missionary presence may also be seen in the question of the eleven cattle which the chiefs had given to the mission in 1879. In June 1879 Koyi and the Scottish artisan Miller had gone up from Kaning'ina to M'mbelwa's village of Echigodhlweni to be formally welcomed by the Ngoni. Part of this welcome involved the gift of eleven cattle to the mission.[45] Gifts of individual cattle to important guests were reasonably common in Ngoni society. For example, both M'mbelwa and Mtwalo gave a cow to the mission in 1878, and Mzukuzuku gave one in March 1879.[46] It would seem however, that the gift of cattle in June 1879 had a far greater symbolic significance than has generally been recognized. Several factors point to this conclusion.

First, in spite of internal disagreements among the Ngoni at this time, it is clear from the speeches made during the welcome that the chiefs regarded the occasion as of considerable importance, and were making a real effort to present a united front.[47] Secondly, the gift of eleven cattle, rather than. one or two, is a clear indication of the seriousness with which the Ngoni regarded the occasion. Thirdly, the Ngoni at first insisted on keeping the cattle in *uNgoni*, and in July Miller had to go up from Kaning'ina to build a kraal for them, most probably at M'mbelwa's village.[48] Fourthly, the physical transfer of the cattle to the mission took place only after the mission had

---

[43] Ibid., 11 August 1884.

[44] Ibid., Sutherland to Laws, 23 December 1884.

[45] Kaning'ina Journal, 12 June 1879, Ms. 7910, NLS.

[46] W.P. Livingstone, *Laws of Livingstonia*, 156; & Bandawe Journal, 1 April 1879, Ms. 7910, NLS.

[47] Kaning'ina Journal, 12 June 1879, Ms. 7910, NLS.

[48] *Ibid.*, 5 July 1879.

settled permanently at Njuyu in 1882;[49] and fifthly, continued Ngoni references to the gift as late as 1887 make it clear that they regarded the transfer as an event of considerable significance. These Ngoni references suggest that they regarded the gift as a pledge of friendship - not in an ordinary sense, but in a mystical and binding way. In many respects the gift bore strong resemblances to the transfer of the *lobola* cattle on the arrangement of an Ngoni marriage, and the Ngoni certainly spoke of the relationship of M'mbelwa and the mission in these terms. Furthermore, the Ngoni feared that unless the mission clearly acknowledged acceptance of the gift, and its consequences (in their view) of a mission-Ngoni alliance,[50] then other tribes would be encouraged to attack them. Once the cattle had been accepted, on the other hand, their safety became a mission responsibility, and as late as 1887, M'mbelwa warned the Lovedale evangelist George Williams that 'your safety and the safety of all the missionaries depended upon the keeping of the cattle that was given to Dr. Laws.'[51]

Though William Koyi himself was not entirely clear about the precise significance of the gift, he did recognize that it was of considerable symbolic importance, and urged Laws to be cautious in respect of it.[52] In retrospect it would seem that the gift was a symbolic gesture of considerable significance, perhaps representing a mystical marriage between the Ngoni and the mission, and that Koyi's sensitive handling of the situation at this very early stage may have helped to ensure Ngoni acceptance of the missionary presence at a time when some elements in the Ngoni leadership would have preferred confrontation.

Initially, the cattle had been kept at M'mbelwa's village, but, in August 1882, the Ngoni allowed the cattle to be transferred to a specially built kraal at Njuyu. This may indicate that they were beginning to see the mission presence as more permanent, but their confidence was certainly not something which could be taken for granted, and was something which Koyi, in particular, knew had to be continually cultivated.

For most Ngoni at this point of their relations with the mission, there was no question of conversion to another religion—indeed, the whole concept of conversion would probably have seemed odd. For some, the missionaries could be useful allies against the Tonga, for others, they could be regarded as dispensers of alternative forms of spiritual power—as in the case of praying

[49] Koyi to Laws, 26 August 1882, Shepperson Collection.
[50] Kaning'ina Journal, 24 June 1879, Ms. 7910, NLS.
[51] Williams to Laws, 21 September 1887, Ms. 7890, NLS.
[52] Koyi to Laws, 13 September 1882, Shepperson Collection.

for rain or good crops. For a few younger Ngoni, however, especially around Hoho and Njuyu, the constant contact with Koyi and his ideas (undoubtedly helped also by the gainful employment he provided) began to have its effect in a more direct way. This was especially the case with the three Tembo brothers, Mawelera, Makara and Chitezi, who became Koyi's helpers, and, in some respects at least, his pupils. Surprisingly, these first three potential converts were the sons of a traditional doctor Kalengo Tembo, who seems to have been well disposed towards the mission. Two of the three, Mawelera and Makara, were to go on to become (in April 1890, and after further instruction from Elmslie) the first two Ngoni to be baptised as Christians. It was, however, their relationship with William Koyi which set them on the road to conversion.

Ngoni Christian Music

In one particular respect Koyi's work with the Tembo brothers is worthy of note—the area of African Christian music. Often, in such pioneer situations, linguistic difficulties, and the absence of any appropriate indigenous hymnody, led to rather stolid early translations of European hymns into the vernacular. There are some elements of this common pattern discernible in the slightly later interaction between the Ngoni and W.A. Elmslie—the first Scottish missionary really to master their language. In 1886, Elmslie published *Izongoma zo'Mlungu* (the first printed book in siNgoni). It included the ten commandments, the Lord's prayer, and several short scripture portions, as well as fourteen European hymns translated by Elmslie himself. These hymns included such late nineteenth century favourites as 'Just as I am', 'O Come all ye Faithful' and 'Hallelujah what a Saviour'.[53] Several years before this event, however, a different and much more contextualised tradition had already begun to take root among the Ngoni.

As early as June 1883, Koyi makes mention of the fact that the Tembo brothers are helping him with singing, and implies also that they are moving around with him as he travels about to hold services.[54] Yet various correspondence by Koyi at this time, makes it clear that he was doing more than merely introducing the Ngoni youths to translations of English hymns. To begin with, Koyi was using Xhosa and Zulu hymns which he had brought from the Cape. Some of these undoubtedly may have been translations of English hymns, but they would probably have been much better translations than those that Elmslie was soon to produce. In addition, the development of

---

[53] W.A. Elmslie, Hymns: *Izongoma zo'Mlungu*, Blantyre, 1886.
[54] Koyi to Laws, 21 June 1883, Shepperson collection, EUL.

a tradition of indigenous hymn writing means that at least some of these compositions were African, rather than mere translations. In particular, John Knox Bokwe at Lovedale, Koyi's most faithful correspondent during his time in Malawi, was himself a prolific composer in a variety of styles, [55] and sent some of his compositions to Koyi in Malawi. Thus, at a very early stage of the development of Christianity among the Ngoni—indeed well before any Ngoni were technically Christians at all—William Koyi was introducing them to a tradition of indigenous African Christian music—a tradition which was to flower in the years after his death.

The Ngoni themselves had a very strong tradition of indigenous music, expressed in a number of different forms—most notably praise songs to the chief, and songs for war, weddings, and children. In the years which were to follow Mawelera Tembo, one of the three brothers who were Koyi's first followers, became one of the most prolific writers of indigenous Christian hymns, sometimes melding traditional tunes to new Christian words, sometimes composing completely new tunes and words. Originally such hymns were composed in siNgoni, but as they became popular throughout a much wider area (and as more and more of the younger generation of Ngoni Christians began to speak the chiTumbuka language of the people among whom they had settled) many of these hymns began to be translated into other local languages—and, beyond that, eventually finding their way not only into English translations in Malawi, but even into international hymn-books in Europe and North America. The most recent of these international compilations, *Come Let us Walk this Road Together: 43 Songs from Africa*, published in America in 1997, contains one of Mawelera Tembo's hymns, written to a traditional Ngoni dance tune around a century ago. [56]

A good deal of the credit for the development of an authentic Ngoni hymnody must undoubtedly go to William Koyi for his early encouragement of indigenous music. He was fortunate to have such promising material to work with—Mawelera Tembo, for example, remained throughout his life an expert on traditional Ngoni music, and when the English anthropologist Margaret Read was compiling lists of very old Ngoni songs in the 1930s, Mawelera Tembo (who lived until 1937) was one of her main informants. [57]

---

[55] *Lovedale Past and Present*, 22-24, and *Dictionary of South African Biography*, Vol. 1, 88-89.

[56] Tom Colvin, *Come Let us Walk this Road Together: 43 Songs from Africa*, Hope Publishing Company, Carol Stream, Illinois, 1997.

[57] See, for example, Margaret Read, 'Songs of the Ngoni People' in *Bantu Studies*, XI(1), 1937.

Undoubtedly too, the interest and encouragement of the Scottish missionary Donald Fraser in the late 1890s and early 1900s helped to consolidate and authenticate the indigenous tradition of Christian composition.[58] When the first official hymn-book of what is now the Livingstonia synod of the Church of Central Africa, Presbyterian (which included the northern Ngoni area) was published in 1910, Fraser's chairmanship of the organising committee ensured the inclusion of many Ngoni hymns. But the origin of the tradition (even in its Christian form) long predates Fraser's arrival in Malawi in 1897. By then there had already taken root a strong tradition of Ngoni Christian composition, whose origins may be jointly traced to the traditional Ngoni love of and talent for music, and the encouragement of William Koyi at the embryonic stage of Ngoni Christian development.

William Koyi's Significance

Throughout these years it would be no exaggeration to say that William Koyi was the most important outsider living among the Ngoni. No important meeting involving the Ngoni and any non-African group could take place without him being present. This was partly due to his linguistic ability, of course; but the explanation was wider than that. The Ngoni trusted Koyi, and, though they recognised that he was not quite one of themselves, they saw him as an intermediary—a concept to which we will return a little later.

Koyi had, of course, been part of the first ever meeting between the missionaries and M'mbelwa in December 1878, when Alexander Riddel, still suffering the after-effects of fever, had defined the purpose of the mission's presence among the Ngoni in a way which they interpreted in largely military and economic terms.[59] He was present also when Laws (accompanied by Frederick Moir of the newly formed Livingstonia Central Africa Trading Company) first met M'mbelwa in January 1879,[60] and again, when Moir's brother John made what may be considered the first specifically commercial visit of a European to M'mbelwa in July 1879.[61] More problematically, perhaps (in terms of the trust in which the Ngoni held Koyi) was his presence at the first ever visit of a British colonial official to M'mbelwa on 18th April 1885, when Lawrence Goodrich, British acting consul 'in the territories of

[58] Thompson, *Christianity in Northern Malawi*, 147-51.
[59] Kaning'ina Journal, 20 December 1878, NLS 7910.
[60] Laws to Thomas Main, 26 March 1879, NLS 7876.
[61] Notes by John W. Moir, 'Mombera's to the Basenga Country', NLS 7904.

the African Kings and Chiefs in the districts adjacent to Lake Nyassa' paid his first visit to M'mbelwa.[62]

It would be easy to conclude that Koyi's function at these initial meetings (and at the large number of subsequent contacts) was merely that of an interpreter. It is certainly the case that he played this role, and that without it, the meetings would have been very much more difficult. As Laws had remarked of him, he was 'an interpreter whose heart was thoroughly in what was being said'.[63] Yet it is clear that for the Ngoni William Koyi was much more than merely an interpreter. Shortly after his death in 1886, the Ngoni asked Elmslie who was to be the missionaries' *umteteleli* now that Koyi was dead. Elmslie, in communicating the conversation to Laws, translated *umteteleli* as 'the one for speaking between us'. He seemed quite annoyed that the Ngoni insisted on such a person, and continued 'They must have such an one even though I could make them understand but they won't do so being so long accustomed to Mr. Koyi's ways.'[64] The truth was, of course, that it was not so much the Ngoni who had become accustomed to Koyi's ways, as Koyi who had understood and co-operated with the ways of the Ngoni.

For the Ngoni, Koyi was almost certainly seen as the *mlomo wenkosi* (the mouth of the chief)—the chief in this case being Robert Laws; not simply an interpreter—more like an ambassador. In fact, the meaning of the word *umteteleli* is similar to, though deeper than this. Its basic meaning is an advocate or an intercessor—someone who speaks on your behalf, or in your defence. It can mean 'one who gives judgment for', or even 'one who forgives' in the sense of someone who has the authority and power to settle a case.[65]

There is a further interesting use of the word *umteteleli* in the Xhosa Bible published in 1879, and which William Koyi almost certainly carried back with him when he returned from Lovedale in 1881 to settle among the Ngoni. Here *umteteleli* is used to translate the Greek word *parakletos* used in the gospel of John for the Holy Spirit, and in the first epistle of John for Jesus Christ.[66] In both cases the meaning of the word is 'intercessor' or 'advocate'. When the Ngoni used the word of Koyi, they were not, of course, using it in a Christian theological sense. However, the fact that the

---

[62] Goodrich to Secretary of State for Foreign Affairs (No.3), 24 April 1885, C.O. 525/3, PRO.

[63] Letter of Laws, 17 July 1882, published in *Free Church of Scotland Monthly*, November 1882, 324-5

[64] Elmslie to Laws, 5 November 1886, Shepperson papers, EUL.

[65] See, for example, Döhne, J.L., *A Zulu-Kafir Dictionary*, Cape Town, 1857, 342, and Colenso, J.W., *Zulu-English Dictionary*, Durban, 1884, 548.

[66] *Incwadi Yezibalo Ezingwele*, London 1879; John 14 vv. 16 & 26, I John, 2v.1.

translators of the Xhosa Bible chose to use the same word to translate *parakletos* indicates the depth and importance of the relationship which the word *umteteleli* conveys.

The high regard in which Koyi was held by the Ngoni was not simply due to his work as an advocate for (or mouthpiece of) the missionaries. In the four and a half years between his settling at Njuyu, and his death there, Koyi worked steadily on a number of fronts which built up his reputation among the Ngoni. One of the less spectacular (but perhaps more important) was what we might call the pastoral front. He spent a lot of time travelling between the villages of the various Ngoni chiefs and headmen, visiting them and chatting to them, as well as consoling them at times of sickness and death.[67] At a time when there was a considerable amount of tension between different factions within the Ngoni hierarchy, and between different Ngoni chiefs (for example M'mbelwa and Mtwalo) Koyi's itineration, and concern to make friends with all the Ngoni chiefs was much more important than it might at first appear.

In the first two years of his stay amongst the Ngoni, William Koyi built up a considerable reputation (both with the Ngoni themselves, and with his missionary colleagues) as a man of considerable importance and weight. On several occasions, when M'mbelwa wanted to consult the missionaries on a number of issues, it was not for the Scots, but for the Xhosa Koyi that he sent. To some extent, especially in the early days of contact, this was a matter of linguistic competence; but as late as November 1884 (when Koyi returned to uNgoni with his wife) it was he, and not Sutherland (who had been resident among the Ngoni for over two years) that M'mbelwa summoned to discuss the question of school-work among the Ngoni.[68] Yet at the very time when his influence might be seen to be at its height, the arrival of three newcomers in uNgoni between late 1883 and early 1885 had, in different ways, a deep effect upon his work and confidence.

New Arrivals

The first of these arrivals was George Williams, the one and only new recruit from Lovedale actually to make it to Malawi since the original Lovedale party in 1876. At first sight Williams' arrival at Bandawe on Christmas Eve 1883, and his move up into uNgoni early in 1884, ought to have provided Koyi with much needed companionship (the lack of which he had been

---

[67] See, for example, Koyi to Laws, April 1883, Shepperson Papers, EUL
[68] Sutherland to Laws, 23 December 1884, Shepperson collection, EUL.

lamenting in April 1883).[69] In one particular respect, however, the arrival of Williams created a new source of discontent for Koyi. This was the question of salary, about which there had been a good deal of dispute between Stewart, Laws and the Livingstonia Committee, while Koyi and Ntintili were waiting to return to Malawi. In April 1881, the Livingstonia committee had fixed the salary of the returning Xhosa missionaries (then expected to be Koyi and Ntintili) at £100 per year without rations.[70] (In spite of this minute there seems to have been some confusion about the exact amount which Koyi received on his return. It would seem that he ended up with £105 per annum.)[71]

In spite of several references indicating that George Williams was originally employed on the same terms as Koyi, at their meeting of 2nd May 1884, the Livingstonia committee *confirmed* Williams' salary as £130 per annum[72] (suggesting that this was the amount that he had been receiving). Whatever the precise timing, it is clear that, from shortly after his arrival in uNgoni Williams was earning at least £25 per year more than the experienced Koyi, who was so annoyed about the situation that he wrote to Dr. Scott at Bandawe about the matter sometime in the first half of 1884.[73] (Laws was then on leave in Scotland). Throughout his career, William Koyi had never been one to complain about money, but it is clear that this particular situation caused him a good deal of unhappiness, and led him to an uncharacteristic outburst of protest. Indeed his protest did not end there, for he wrote also to Laws in Scotland complaining about the differential. In a letter which contained both African analogy, and quotation from the poetry of Robert Burns, Koyi told Laws a long involved story about an old horse at Lovedale called Jack—the moral being that you shouldn't treat old horses worse than you treat young ones. Koyi went on:

> Money is not the thing that I like speaking about from the first. But I am only making these few remarks about it this time. In one whey (*sic*) I know well that my schooling is very poor, but for all that a man is a man for all that.[74]

This letter seems to have had a considerable effect, for when the Livingstonia committee met on 7th October 1884, they heard a very favourable report by letter from Dr. Scott at Bandawe on the work of William Koyi, and

---

[69] Koyi to Laws, April 1883, Shepperson collection, EUL

[70] Minutes of Livingstonia sub-committee, 4 April 1881, Ms. 7912, NLS.

[71] Ibid., 26 June 1883.

[72] Ibid., 2 May 1884.

[73] Scott to Laws, 17 July 1884, Acc. 9220 (i) (ii), NLS.

[74] Koyi to Laws, undated, Shepperson collection, EUL.

accepted a recommendation from Laws (who was present at the meeting) that Koyi's salary should be increased to £130 per annum—thus bringing him into line with the much better educated (but much less experienced) Williams, and putting both Xhosa evangelists only slightly behind the two Scottish artisans McCallum and Rollo, who each received £150 per annum.[75]

Part of the reason for Koyi's uncharacteristic complaints, may have been his continuing worry about his wife, who had still not arrived in Malawi by the middle of 1884. It would seem that her delay was based on a mixture of bad health, and reluctance to venture into the totally unknown. However, by the middle of 1884, she was finally ready to set out for Malawi. She travelled north from the Cape with a Nigerian woman, Jane Bissett,[76] who had been studying at Lovedale, and who was coming north to marry Kagasso Sazuze who had also been trained at Lovedale, and had returned to Malawi a few months earlier together with George Williams and Joseph Bismarck. Sazuze then went to work at Zomba for the Church of Scotland mission.

The journey north of Mrs. Koyi and Jane Bissett was not a straightforward one. After reaching Quelimane and starting up the Zambezi, they became caught up in what the *Christian Express* called 'the war troubles on the Zambezi'.[77] The disturbances led to their having to endure 'a month's siege in a sort of stockade near the Dutch Opium Factory'.[78] The siege ended in a pitched battle, in which (according to some accounts) more than one hundred men were killed. It cannot have been a very encouraging start for a woman who was probably very nervous about the enterprise in the first place.

William Koyi had gone south to meet his wife, and probably made contact with her at Katunga's on the Shire river. From there (together with Jane Bissett) they travelled to Blantyre, and, after resting there, went on to Matope, where they caught the *Ilala*, which took them north to Bandawe, where they arrived late in October. After a short rest there, they moved on into uNgoni—arriving at Njuyu on 2nd November 1884.[79]

Under different circumstances, the arrival of his wife might well have made William Koyi's position at Njuyu more pleasant and secure—not only

[75] Minutes of Livingstonia sub-committee, 7 October 1884, and 24 December 1884, Ms. 7912, NLS.

[76] Koyi to Laws, 27 November 1883, Shepperson collection, EUL.

[77] *Christian Express*, January 1885, 5.

[78] *Ibid.*

[79] Letter from W.A. Elmslie, 21 October 1884, *Free Church of Scotland Monthly*, February 1885; Scott to Laws, 30 October 1884, and Sutherland to Laws, 23 December 1884, Acc. 9220 (i) (ii), NLS.

in personal terms, but also in terms of his standing amongst the Ngoni as a married man. Unfortunately the opposite seems to have been the case. From the very beginning of her stay amongst the Ngoni, Mrs. Koyi does not seem to have settled well. The very first news of her arrival commented, 'She is afraid of consumption, otherwise she is pretty well'.[80] We do not, unfortunately, have her own record of how she felt about life among the Ngoni, but, if the reports of others are to be believed (and the record from several different sources is remarkably consistent) her genuine fear of ill health, and her inability to adjust to the difficult and spartan living conditions of the isolated mission station, soon began to have a negative effect on the morale of Koyi himself.

She had arrived at the beginning of the wet season—the worst possible time to try to settle into a new tropical environment. It is clear that her underlying health was not good. Within a few months Dr. Scott from Bandawe was reporting to Laws in Scotland that Mrs. Koyi was never very well, and was very thin; that he had examined her and found that her right lung was partly destroyed. He added that he hadn't told either of them, as 'the mere mention of the fact would send Mrs. Koyi away ... to the South'.[81] By the following month Dr. Elmslie was reporting that she had acute bronchitis. He added that she had never settled in the area, and that she was pressurising Koyi to take her back to the Cape.[82] At exactly the same time an entry in the mission journal at Bandawe was recording very similar news, adding that Koyi did not consider his wife fit for the country, and that she didn't want to stay.[83]

The question of his wife's health and mental attitude was clearly having its effect on William Koyi. In the same letter in which Elmslie reported her acute bronchitis, he also noted 'Mr. Koyi has not a pleasant time with her and it is visibly affecting him so that the natives ask why he is so *morose* now'.[84] Laws, still at home in Scotland in mid-1885, was hoping that Koyi would open a new station among Chikusi's southern Ngoni.[85] (This was the group about which he had commented to his friend Mapassa Ntintili as long ago as 1878 'If then, I am spared to return, I fear I will leave you at Livingstonia, for though I may be nothing there, I am recognised as something

---

[80] Ibid.
[81] Scott to Laws, 29 May 1885, Acc. 9220 (i) (iii), NLS.
[82] Ibid., Elmslie to Laws, 9 June 1885.
[83] Bandawe journal, 5 June 1885, Ms. 7911, NLS.
[84] Ibid., Elmslie to Laws, 9 June 1885, Acc. 9220 9 (i) (iii).
[85] Ibid.

here! I found brethren and sisters here among the Bangoni.')[86] With his wife in such poor health it was clearly out of the question for Koyi to move to a new part of Malawi, and start a new mission station from scratch. It was as much as he could do to persuade his wife to remain at Njuyu.

On top of these worries about her health, during her first few months in Malawi Koyi had also to contend with a very unstable political situation amongst the Ngoni, over the wet season of 1884-85. It may be remembered that he had been reluctant to leave uNgoni in the middle of 1884, and when he actually did so in August, at the beginning of his journey south to meet his wife, the Ngoni were very suspicious of his leaving (for reasons not entirely clear George Williams also left to go down to Bandawe at the same time) and, though two Europeans remained in uNgoni, the rumour spread that Koyi had left finally, and would not be coming back.[87]

After his return, relations continued to be strained for some time. This was due, not so much to Koyi's movements, as to internal tensions within Ngoni society itself. This took various forms: rivalry between M'mbelwa and Mtwalo; arguments between the paramount chief, and those who felt alliance with the mission was bringing them no advantage, and that they should resume a more active policy of raiding the lakeshore—a feeling which surfaced even amongst the Nhlanes (the oldest and most loyal supporters of the mission).[88] The result was that the wet season of 1885-86 proved to be one of the most difficult since Njuyu had first been opened. Both Koyi's correspondence, and reports in the Bandawe Journal indicate a considerable increase in the level of raiding—a development which M'mbelwa seemed unable (or unwilling) to stop.[89]

Thus William Koyi, by the middle of 1885, was facing one of the most trying periods of his entire missionary career, confronted, as he was, not merely with a difficult political situation and the growing cynicism of at least some sections of the Ngoni, but also with the chronic ill-health of his wife, and her desire to return to South Africa. In the short term at least, he seems to have persuaded his wife to stay on. By September he was writing to Robert Laws in Scotland, 'She had fever and a bad cough which put fear into me as it was much what I have seen in the country before in [the] case of S.

---

[86] Letter from Koyi to Ntintili, quoted in *Christian Express*, December 1878, 9.

[87] Sutherland to Laws, 23 December 1884, Shepperson collection, EUL.

[88] George Williams to Laws, undated, quoted in *Free Church of Scotland Monthly*, May 1885, 141.

[89] See, for example, Bandawe Journal, 1 November 1883, quoted in *Free Church of Scotland Monthly*, May 1884, 139.

Mngunana'.[90] Most of Koyi's missionary colleagues, especially the medically trained, might well have shared his fear for the health and very life of his wife. Neither he nor they were then to realise, that it would be he, rather than his wife, who, within a few months, would succumb to much the same symptoms as his Xhosa colleague Mngunana had done in 1877.

In the meantime, the arrival of a third newcomer to uNgoni was, even more than the coming of either George Williams or Koyi's wife, to have a profound effect on the last period of Koyi's service there. The third immigrant was Walter Angus Elmslie, a medical missionary from Aberdeen, who arrived at Njuyu on 21st February 1885.[91] Up until then, apart from Koyi himself, Njuyu had been staffed sporadically by Scottish artisans. As has been pointed out above, these men, such as Sutherland and McCallum, had had a high respect for Koyi, and had often listened to his advice. At the very least, in terms of missionary practice (if not of policy) one might say of this period that in uNgoni Koyi was first among equals. That situation changed radically with the arrival of Elmslie, who, though he was not (at this period) an ordained minister, was a well-educated medical doctor, and was clearly regarded by the mission from the time of his arrival as the missionary in charge of the work in uNgoni. Some indication of the hierarchical structures which were just beginning by this period to develop in the mission, may be gleaned by a discussion which took place at the Livingstonia committee in Scotland just a year after the arrival of Elmslie in uNgoni. Laws was preparing to return to Malawi after his leave, and asked the advice of the committee about the setting-up of a mission council—a body which, for the next seventy years would be the main policy-making structure of the mission in Malawi. In particular, Laws sought advice on the membership of the proposed body. Though precise details were left to him, the committee advised that 'it should include only ordained and medical missionaries'.[92] Thus, until well into the twentieth century, when the composition was gradually changed, the real decisions of the mission were effectively taken by a small group of ordained and medically trained men, and the vast majority of those who worked for the mission—women, artisans, teachers and local Christians—were effectively excluded from its major decision-making body.

Whether it was the worry and uncertainty caused by his wife's illness, or, more directly, the possibly intimidating presence of Elmslie, there is no

---

[90] Koyi to Laws, 5 September 1885, Shepperson collection, EUL.

[91] Letter from Elmslie, 29 May 1885, quoted in *Free Church of Scotland Monthly*, October 1885, 299.

[92] Minutes of the Livingstonia sub-committee, 27 April 1886, Ms. 7912, NLS.

doubt that the tenor of Koyi's letters changed considerably from about this time onwards. Whereas his earlier letters to Laws (as has been noted above) had been natural, chatty, and quite prepared to give advice, his later letters seem much more hesitant and lacking in confidence. It was not that Elmslie treated him particularly harshly, or that the two men got on badly together. Neither was the case; but Elmslie, in spite of his initial lack of experience and linguistic competence, very quickly began to assert his own authority over Koyi and Williams—as well as the Scottish artisans.

To a considerable extent it is certainly true that Elmslie respected Koyi, and the work he had done. Certainly, in comparison to his opinion of Williams Elmslie thought highly of Koyi, and when, at the end of the century, he wrote his book *Among the Wild Ngoni* he contributed a whole chapter to the memory of his Xhosa colleague.[93] Yet one must clearly distinguish between Elmslie's appreciation of Koyi's personal qualities, and his sometimes very harsh criticisms of the way in which Koyi (and even more so, his compatriot Williams) related to Ngoni culture. Elmslie, particularly in the early days of his service in Malawi, was not very sympathetic to many aspects of traditional Ngoni culture, and it was often when Koyi appeared to be most in tune with it that Elmslie's criticisms of him were most forthright. Yet, more generally, it has to be borne in mind that Elmslie, by inclination, was a very critical person. In one letter, for example, written in January 1886 to his friend Alexander Roberts, who was teaching at Lovedale, he was highly critical , not only of the Xhosa evangelists (and Mrs. Koyi) but also of some of his Scottish colleagues, including James Sutherland (who had been a mutual friend of his and Roberts, and who had died at Bandawe a few months earlier in September 1885) and of Dr. Scott, who had been acting head of the mission during Laws' leave in Scotland.[94] On subsequent occasions he was highly critical of many of his other Scottish colleagues.

In January 1886, however, in a highly personal letter to Roberts, it was the Xhosa who took the brunt of his criticism. In a sweeping condemnation which was clearly racist, Elmslie told Roberts:

> This station will be served by Europeans. I would have no more Kaffirs. They are not far enough removed from the idea of all natives that they need to see

---

[93] W.A. Elmslie, *Among the Wild Ngoni*, Edinburgh, 1899, chapter IX, 'In Memoriam: William Koyi'

[94] Elmslie to Roberts, 28 January 1886, Roberts' papers, PR 3515(a), Cory Library, Rhodes University.

their friends about every three months. I enjoy working with them, but I do not like to hear so much about their sacrifices in staying here.[95]

In a sense this criticism points to Elmslie's almost total inability to see things from an African perspective. His greatest criticisms of Koyi, for example, occurred in those areas of interaction with Ngoni culture which constitute the very essence of Koyi's contribution to the laying of the foundations of a Ngoni Christianity, but which Elmslie viewed only as an aberration from European norms. Only a few months after arriving in the country, Elmslie criticised Koyi for getting too close to the Ngoni:

> Mr. Koyi's ability to know the people is invaluable but there is not that weight with him which a white man carries. There is a danger in knowing the people too well and while Koyi is invaluable here, there is not that respect shown to him which should be and which is a factor in raising the people from their low condition.[96]

In particular, Elmslie was critical of Koyi for his generosity in giving presents. Writing after Koyi's death (and in a letter which, on balance was favourable to Koyi) Elmslie nevertheless felt it necessary to remark:

> Mr. Koyi gave on his own showing £20 every year in presents and to-day in any quarter you will find that this fact, and not the Gospel he preached, is what the natives remember.[97]

If that criticism were ever true—and I doubt it—it is certainly not the case to-day.

Elmslie also criticised Koyi on the same ground on several earlier occasions. Before he had even reached uNgoni, for example, he wrote to Laws, accusing Koyi of not resisting the demands of M'mbelwa.[98] Clearly this was information he had picked up from other Scottish missionaries at Bandawe. It is undoubtedly true that Koyi (and his Xhosa compatriot Williams) were more generous in their giving of gifts to the Ngoni than Elmslie or most of the other Scottish missionaries were. Several things need to be said about this. In the first place, both Koyi and Williams were far more aware of the importance of gift-giving in Ngoni and Xhosa culture, than were the Scottish missionaries. They recognised that giving generous gifts helped to establish the importance and credibility of the giver, and that it might well be a factor in developing friendly attitudes towards the mission.

---

[95] Ibid.

[96] Elmslie to Laws, 9 June 1885, Shepperson collection, EUL.

[97] Elmslie to Laws, 10 August 1887, Ms. 7890, NLS.

[98] Elmslie to Laws, 29 January 1885 (addendum of 12 February), Livingstonia papers, Acc. 9220(I) (iii), NLS.

On the negative side, there were occasions when Koyi was under considerable pressure—sometimes even physical pressure—to be more generous towards the Ngoni. On one occasion, for example, when Koyi had employed eight Ngoni to help him break in a team of oxen, a dispute broke out about how much they should be paid. The leader of the group, Magoda Nhlane, physically threatened Koyi with a spear and a club. Although the intervention of Chipatula's wife prevented violence, Koyi ended up having to pay more than he wanted for the work done.[99] Thirdly, Elmslie seems to have failed to take account of the two-way nature of gifts. Clearly, the Ngoni were eager, especially in the early days, to obtain trade goods, such as cloth, from contact with the missionaries, and to do so at the lowest possible cost; but they, in their turn, gave gifts to the missionaries. The most notable of these was the gift of eleven cattle, but there were many other examples. Chiputula gave Koyi a gift of food on more than one occasion—for example, the gift of a pumpkin, two jars of milk, and some green maize. On another occasion, Koyi records that when the Ngoni found him hoeing in his field, they took the hoe from him, and did the work for him themselves.[100] In summary, Elmslie seems to have assessed the question of giving gifts in narrowly economic terms; Koyi and the Ngoni saw it much more in terms of social relationships.

It would be wrong, however, to suggest that Elmslie's attitude to Koyi was predominantly negative. It was not, and, as we have seen above, on many occasions the medical missionary had positive things to say about Koyi, and his contribution to the work of the mission among the Ngoni.

Missionary Rain-makers

Early in 1886 a major crisis occurred in uNgoni. This was brought about by the failure of the rains, and the fear of a major drought. For several weeks all of the missionaries working among the Ngoni (but predominantly Elmslie and Koyi) were under considerable pressure—both physical and psychological. In his later book *Among the Wild Ngoni*[101] Elmslie devoted a whole chapter to the crisis.

After a few showers in November 1885, the rains stopped, and for the next seven weeks—a crucial period in the agricultural year—absolutely no rain fell. After the apparent failure of traditional sacrifices, some elements of

---

[99] Sutherland to Laws, 13 September 1882, Shepperson collection, EUL.

[100] Letter from William Koyi, quoted in *Christian Express*, 2 April 1883, 1.

[101] W.A. Elmslie, *Among the Wild Ngoni*, Edinburgh, Oliphant Anderson & Ferrier, 1899, 320pp.

the Ngoni began blaming the missionaries for withholding the rain.[102] A group of M'mbelwa's councillors, accompanied by an army which Elmslie estimated at one hundred and sixty, came to try to persuade Elmslie to go across to the chief's village to pray for rain there. He refused, because, as he later explained:

> We wanted the people to come to our service on the station, and did not wish the Bible to be over at the chief's on such an occasion, because they attached a superstitious importance to the Book.[103]

While Elmslie's later published account of the crisis does mention its seriousness, there is little of the emotional tension which can be felt in his contemporary accounts. In a letter to his friend A.W. Roberts at Lovedale, Elmslie says 'I had my brace of revolvers loaded, two rifles and my fowling piece', and to the Scots missionary Kerr Cross he writes, 'You would have seen every gun in the station lying loaded that night.'[104]

The night in question was Saturday 16 January. The missionaries seriously thought they might be attacked during the night—due mainly to what they considered the aggressive and intimidating behaviour of the Ngoni army which had carried out a war dance on the road near the missionaries' houses at Njuyu. In the event, no attack took place. The following day, being a Sunday, the usual weekly service was held at Njuyu. Though we have only Elmslie's account of what was said, in fact, William Koyi played a prominent part. He led the service, spoke about the ten commandments, and translated Elmslie's sermon.[105] Prayers were said for rain, and it is possible that these too were said (or at least translated) by William Koyi.

There are small, but significant variations in Elmslie's different accounts of the events. Several of the accounts seem to indicate that Elmslie was opposed in principle to going to the chief's village to pray for rain, but his letter to Roberts includes the sentence, 'We had before this [the arrival of the war party] agreed to go to Mombera's [M'mbelwa's] next day to have a meeting.'[106] This small variation is significant, for his letter to Roberts contains another sentence which appears nowhere else in his accounts. This is put in the form of a question from one of M'mbelwa's indunas. 'Could we hold special meetings at the head kraal as was done two years ago?'[107] The

---

[102] Elmslie to Roberts, 28 January 1886, Roberts' papers, Cory library, Rhodes university.
[103] Elmslie, *Wild Ngoni*, 173.
[104] Ibid.
[105] Elmslie, *Wild Ngoni*, 175-6.
[106] Elmslie to Roberts, 28 January 1886.
[107] Ibid.

relevance of this is that, as we have already seen, William Koyi had gone to M'mbelwa's village to pray for good crops—essentially, at that time of year to pray for rain—in December 1882. This was actually three years previously, so it is possible that, though we have no record of the fact, Koyi may have done the same in December 1883 or January 1884. The extremely large attendance which Koyi mentions for the December 1882 meeting can indicate only one thing—that the Ngoni regarded the occasion, not as a routine service of the new religion, but as a traditional ritual of considerable national importance.[108] That Koyi was willing to carry out such rituals—and presumably with some success— would have meant that by the time of the crisis in January 1886, and whether Elmslie was aware of it or not, the Ngoni were already regarding the missionaries as rainmakers of considerable power.

On Monday 18 January Elmslie reported that a large crowd had gathered at the chief's village, and were expecting the missionaries to come across and pray for rain. Once again Elmslie refused to go, though a further service was held at Njuyu. Elmslie reported that before the people had dispersed after the meeting, heavy rain had already fallen.[109]

Though Elmslie himself was later to downplay the significance of the events of January 1886 in bringing about a more receptive attitude towards the mission on the part of the Ngoni,[110] it seems more likely that it confirmed in the minds of the Ngoni that the missionaries were the repositories of major spiritual power, and that co-operation with them was, on balance, more sensible than confrontation. If this were the case, then it is also likely, that M'mbelwa's decision in May 1886 to allow schools to be opened was not unconnected with the missionaries' apparent success in bringing rain in January.

The Death of William Koyi

The decision to allow schools to open, when it came, found William Koyi literally on his death bed. He had never enjoyed particularly good health

---

[108] I have argued elsewhere that the time of year when this took place was exactly the time of year when the Ngoni would have celebrated the *Incwala* feast of first-fruits in South Africa, and that they may have connected the occasion with this. See, Thompson, 'True Love and Roots: a Centenary Re-assessment of the Work of William Koyi among the Ngoni', in *Society of Malawi Journal*, 39(2), 1986, 15-25.

[109] Elmslie, Wild Ngoni, 176.

[110] For example, his statement in a letter to Scotland at the time, that 'I can point to no particular incident closely connected with the happy change in the feelings of the people', quoted in *Among the Wild Ngoni*, 182.

throughout his time in Malawi, and suffered from tuberculosis. In May 1886, following an attack of what seems to have been malaria, but may have been a tuberculous fever, his condition deteriorated rapidly. Elmslie, who had gone to Bandawe, was summoned back to Njuyu, and for a few days Koyi seemed to rally. The improvement was only temporary, however, and on 6th June 1886, William Koyi died from the complications of chronic tuberculosis.[111]

Mrs. Koyi did not remain long in Malawi following her husband's death. As we have seen above her own health had been poor since the time of her arrival in the country, and she had been eager to leave for some time. With the death of Koyi she had no reason to remain. Almost immediately after Koyi's death, she moved from Njuyu to Bandawe, on the lakeshore, to await the next voyage south of the Ilala.[112] By September 1886 she had arrived back in the Eastern Cape, and was staying with her brother, Rev. James van Rooyen, at Uitenhage.[113]

The shock of Koyi's loss was genuine on the part of his colleagues, and fulsome praise for his life and work came from all quarters. James Stewart wrote of 'a personal friend whom I greatly esteemed and loved';[114] even Elmslie, not often given to lavish praise, described Koyi as 'one with whom it was a privilege to associate' and in what to-day would appear as a rather odd and patronising phrase (but which at the time was certainly meant as a generous compliment) commented, 'no white man would have degraded himself if he had taken off his hat to him.'[115]

Obituaries appeared in several mission publications, including the *Christian Express* at Lovedale, and the *Free Church of Scotland Monthly Record* in Glasgow. Without any doubt Koyi's Scottish colleagues thought very highly of him; but they did so for a rather contorted reason—because they saw him as approximating to their own Euro-centric ideas of a civilised Christian gentleman. This has already emerged in some of Elmslie's comments on him; it surfaces also in the obituary in the *Christian Express*, which remarked both that 'He had the quality not common among natives of command over his fellows' and that 'His habits of thought were more those of a European, though never separating himself in his sympathy from his coun-

---

[111] Kerr Cross to Laws, 19 June 1886, and Elmslie to Laws, 6 July 1886, Shepperson collection, EUL.

[112] Kerr Cross to Laws, 19 June 1886, Shepperson collection, EUL.

[113] *Christian Express*, October 1886, 147.

[114] Stewart to Laws, 25 August 1886, Shepperson collection, EUL.

[115] Quoted in J.W. Jack, *Daybreak at Livingstonia*, Edinburgh, 1901, chapter 6, p.21.

trymen.'[116] Inherent in much of this praise was the dilemma of the Lovedale educational ethic, which assumed that no real progress could be made until Africans largely abandoned their traditional culture and worldview in favour of a European orientation. Such a view was startlingly expressed by a group of Lovedale graduates themselves (including several who had been associated with the Livingstonia project, such as Isaac Wauchope and Mpambani Mzimba) when, in a letter to James Stewart, they spoke of themselves as 'a people just emerging from a state of barbarism' and praised Lovedale for helping them to 'rise in the scale of civilization'.[117] To what extent such a phrase represented their real feelings on the matter, need not detain us here. What is clear, however, is that William Koyi's significance lay in precisely the opposite direction: his ability to empathise with the Ngoni in a period of rapid social, and, indeed, religious change, while never compromising his own Christian values.

News of Koyi's death reached Lovedale about six weeks after the event. One of the first to learn of it was his friend John Knox Bokwe, who immediately telegrammed Isaac Wauchope,[118] then working as a court interpreter in Port Elizabeth. A few days later an obituary appeared in the *Port Elizabeth Telegraph*, and was later reproduced in the Xhosa newspaper *Imvo Zabantsundu*[119] (which had begun publication in 1884, under the editorship of John Tengo Jabavu—another Lovedale graduate). It is possible that it was written by Wauchope himself, and, if so, he would have drawn on his short but intense experience of Koyi as friend and mentor during those few short months of preparation for and travel to Malawi in 1876.

The obituary reproduced in *Imvo* in both Xhosa and English twice describes Koyi as 'no ordinary man', and it seems that this might also sum up the Ngoni view of him. We have already noted the Ngoni use of the term *umteteleli* with reference to Koyi. The nickname which they gave him, Mtusane (sometimes translated 'the bridge-builder' or 'the go-between')[120] contains something of the same idea—a man who could co-exist in two very different worlds, and represent one to the other. In the extremely delicate, and sometimes dangerous conditions of uNgoni in the 1880s, such a quality was vitally important. Koyi's significance—especially from the perspective of the early growth of Christianity amongst the Ngoni—lay precisely in his

---

[116] 'In Memoriam William Koyi' in *Christian Express*, September 1886, 1.

[117] Quoted in Leon de Kock, *Civilizing Barbarians*, 98.

[118] *Imvo Zabantsundu*, 18 August 1886, 3.

[119] *Ibid.*

[120] See 'A Note on the Names of William Koyi' in this book.

ability to understand both the Ngoni and the missionary perspective simultaneously, and to convince the Ngoni (however slowly and fragmentarily) that alliance with the mission and what it represented was not entirely opposed to their own long-term interests. He did so, not by intellect, but by solidarity: by standing alongside the Ngoni, and becoming (as far as was possible) one of them. Immediately after Koyi's death, the Ngoni described him as 'their special friend'.[121] That such an opinion has endured, and that William Koyi is still widely remembered and respected amongst the Ngoni to-day, well over a century after his death, is a clear indication of just how important his contribution was.

---

[121] Letter of Elmslie, 25 June 1886, quoted in *Christian Express*, February 1887, 24.

Praise Song for Mtusane

This poem, which I composed for my book *Touching the Heart*, is written in the style of a Ngoni praise song to a hero. Such songs are full of analogy and symbolism. The main analogies in this poem are explained below.

Builder of bridges across the Kasitu;
Warrior without a spear,
Your courage was your shield.

Strong as a long-horned bull,
Gentle as a suckling cow.
Eagle hovering over Hoho
Wild hare upon the mountains.

Giver of generous gifts
Safe guardian of lobola cattle.
Teacher of songs,
Explainer of the Book,
Bringer of rain upon our fields,
Friend of our dreams.

Right hand of Lobarti
Mouth of the strangers.
Advocate who spoke with mercy.

Opener of the path to the future,
You understood the ways
We feared to leave.

Son of Ngqika
Brother of Zwangendaba;
Your bones still lie near Chipatula's place;
Your spirit runs throughout our land.

Umhlobo wenhloko

The main analogies used in the praise poem are as follows: William Koyi's Ngoni name was Mtusane, one possible meaning of which is 'bridge-builder'. The Kasitu is a river in northern Malawi. The mission station at Njuyu was on the east bank, the chief's village on the west. The Ngoni were great cattle-keeping people. Hoho was the village of Chiputula Nhlane, an induna of the paramount chief M'mbelwa. Lobola was bride-wealth, often given in the form of cattle. Lobarti was the Ngoni name for Robert Laws, leader of the mission. Another of the terms the Ngoni used for Koyi was Umteteleli, which means advocate, or intercessor. Ngqika may be regarded as the father of that branch of the Xhosa people to which Koyi belonged; Zwangendaba was the original leader of the Ngoni. Koyi is buried at Njuyu, near the village of Chiputula Nhlane.

A Note on the Names of William Koyi

Over the more than thirty years that I have been interested in William Koyi, I have sporadically collected information about the different names by which he has been known. Some of this information is scattered throughout several of the essays in this collection; but it may be useful to gather it together here, alongside some new insights that have emerged more recently.

Koyi

First there is Koyi's surname itself. It is not a common name in the Eastern Cape, though there were four other Koyi brothers at Lovedale in the 1870s (unrelated to William).[1] In trying to trace its origins I have encountered several different linguistic possibilities. The word *iKoyi* does exist in Xhosa. It means a crib or a frame for storing maize, or sometimes a small hut used for the same purpose.[2] But it is not a common word, and it is possible that it has been assimilated from Afrikaans. Certainly in modern Dutch the word *kooi* can mean a bunk on a ship, which is similar to the Xhosa meaning of crib. The Dutch form of the word, Kooi, can be used as a surname, so it is at least possible that William Koyi himself (or his ancestors) adopted the name after some association with an Afrikaner family of the same name, eventually africanizing the spelling of Kooi to become Koyi.[3]

In his recent book *The Missionary* the retired South African missionary with Nkhoma Synod of the CCAP, Attie Labuschagne suggests that the name Koyi 'indicates… a blood link with the Khoi-Khoyi'.(sic)[4] No evidence is produced to back up this theory, other than the assertion that many others had such a connection. If that were so you would expect the surname Koyi to be fairly widespread in South Africa; in fact, however, as far as I am aware, it is very rare. Certainly no one I spoke to in South Africa, during my research there for my book *Touching the Heart* mentioned the possibility of the name Koyi indicating a Khoi ethnic origin. In addition most of the early accounts of Koyi's life indicate that he was a member of the Ngqika branch of the Xhosa people.[5] The classic photograph of William Koyi with his

---

[1] *Lovedale Past and Present*, 124.
[2] I am grateful to Dr. R.G. Sipo Makalima of Alice for this information.
[3] I have come across a Hungarian form of the name, actually spelt 'Koyi', but it is unlikely that this is the origin of the Xhosa surname.
[4] A.S. Labuschagne, *The Missionary*, 47.
[5] *Lovedale Past and Present*, 125. In the late nineteenth century 'Ngqika' was usually spelled

Lovedale colleagues, prior to setting out for Malawi in 1876, does not seem to reveal any Khoi features, and on balance, I think, we may leave this possibility aside.

Mtusane

As I have discussed elsewhere[6] there is a great deal of controversy over William Koyi's nickname *Mtusane* which appears to have been given to him by the Ngoni. Various etymological explanations for this have been given, including 'the bridge-builder', 'the go-between' and 'the helper'.[7] The late Fergus Macpherson used to insist that it meant the bridge-builder, but, if it did, it was certainly in a very metaphorical sense which paraphrased the original siNgoni.

Linguistically the word almost certainly comes from the Zulu or Xhosa verb *ukutusa* which has a number of different meanings, including 'to praise, recommend, to speak highly of'. *Mtusane* would appear to be the personal reciprocal form, meaning, 'a person who praises another', or 'one who speaks highly of another'.

Yet very recently, after I had published *Touching the Heart*, I was looking through some of my very old research notes, and I came across an interview I had done with *inkosana* Mopho Jere nearly thirty years ago. While going through this in detail, I discovered that he had a very specific explanation of Koyi's name *Mtusane*. According to Mopho Jere (who was born in 1887, just one year after William Koyi died) *Mtusane* does indeed come from the verb *ukutusa*. He explained *ukutusa* as meaning 'to subjugate anger'. He also thought that the name might have come from South Africa, rather than having been given by the Ngoni; but the more intriguing point lies, I think, in the alternative explanation of the meaning of the word itself. If *ukutusa* does indeed mean 'to subjugate anger' – and this was Mopho Jere's precise definition in English – then a new and attractive possibility opens up. For *Mtusane* would then mean 'the person who puts down anger in another', i.e. 'the peacemaker'. Whether or not the name was given to him by the Ngoni (as most authorities seem to think) or was a name he already had when he came from South Africa (which Mopho Jere suggested) it would be a very appropriate title for someone, who, for most of his missionary career, spent a large amount of his time making and keeping the peace between the Ngoni and the Scottish missionaries.

'Gaika'.
[6] *Touching the Heart*, 133.
[7] *Ibid.*

71

Umteteleli [8]

Strictly speaking *Umteteleli* was not one of William Koyi's nicknames, but rather an explanation of how the Ngoni saw his function. Elmslie, writing to Laws in 1886 reported, 'When Mr. Koyi died several of the councillors came asking who was to be the "Umteteleli" now i.e. the one for speaking between us.'[9] The literal meaning of *umteteleli* is 'an advocate' or 'an intercessor'.[10] Elmslie clearly thought that the word merely meant an interpreter, i.e. someone who could speak siNgoni. He complained, 'They must have such an one even though I could make them understand but they won't do so, being so long accustomed to Mr. Koyi's ways.'[11] As I have pointed out in my book *Touching the Heart* the significance of *umteteleli* is much deeper than merely an interpreter.[12] The Ngoni saw Koyi, I believe, as an ambassador, almost one might say, a defence counsel, who could interpret their ideas, culture, and concerns (not merely their language) to the Scottish missionaries.[13]

Isigidimi

Some years ago, I had become aware that there still existed in Malawi, at least one song about William Koyi, which among other things, had been taught to children at primary school many years ago. It was only during my visit to Malawi in November 2002, however, that I managed to track down some of the words of the song. When I did so, yet another name for William Koyi emerged.

Rev. Howard Matiya Nkhoma, General Secretary of the Livingstonia Synod of the CCAP had first alerted me to the existence of this song some years ago. In November 2002, while in Malawi for the Loudon centenary celebrations, I asked him to sing the snatch of the song which he remembered. He did better than that; he introduced me to his old uncle, Nathan Kaheni Mapunda Banda, who, as a boy, had been taught the song in school,

---

[8] A fuller explanation of this title is given in my article 'William Koyi and the Ngoni', reproduced in this book.

[9] Elmslie to Laws, 5 November 1886, Livingstonia Papers, NLS.

[10] This is the meaning given in J.L. Döhne, *Zulu-Kafir Dictionary*, Cape Town, 1857, 342. My own copy of this early dictionary was the one actually owned by W.A. Elmslie, and before him by Dr. George Steele, an early missionary among the Ngoni, who died in 1895.

[11] Elmslie to Laws, 5 November 1886, NLS.

[12] Thompson, *Touching the Heart*, 118-19.

[13] This is the significance of the phrase 'advocate who spoke with mercy' in my poem 'Praise Song for Mtusane' reproduced in this book.

around the time of the First World War. He too, remembered only one verse. It went as follows:

William Koyi, William Koyi

Sigidini samaXhosa

Wangaruta ku Collegi

Usekulu wa Wazungu

Wati waruta wanguwona

Chikarata kutuliya kwaku Lawsi

Kulembeka Nyasalandi

Immediately I started writing this down, one word stood out as being strange, and not from northern Malawi. However, when I asked Matiya Nkhoma, 'What does "sigidini" mean?' his reply was, 'We don't know; we thought you would know. Did you not use the word in one of your books?'[14] This did not immediately ring any bells with me, but, on returning home I began doing a little linguistic research. If the word was not Tumbuka or Tonga, then the chances were that it was either Ngoni or Xhosa. Consulting a number of different Xhosa and Zulu dictionaries, I discovered that the word was, in fact, from the Zulu-Xhosa cluster of languages. It was not, in its commonest form, **sigidini**[15], but **isigidimi**. And it meant 'a messenger'[16] or 'a runner'. I had used the word several times in my book *Touching the Heart*, for it was the name of a famous Xhosa newspaper in the late nineteenth century: *Isigidimi sama Xosa* (*sic*).

So here, from the song, was yet another nickname for William Koyi: 'the messenger', or 'the messenger of the Xhosa'. At this distance in time it is impossible to be sure how and why the name originated. Any explanation must be speculative. Let us take first the larger phrase, 'Sigidini samaXhosa'. There is a story about William Koyi which appears in the book, *Lovedale Past and Present*[17] and tells how Koyi was working as a store-

---

[14] Informal conversation, Rev. H. Matiya Nkhoma, 1 November 2002.

[15] There are, in fact, several older forms of the term: isigidimi, isigijima etc. so it is possible that the surviving version in the song, is, in fact, a very old form of the word, from the mid-nineteenth century.

[16] My colleague Dr. Andrew Ross, recognised the word in this form as the isiXhosa for the herald of a chief.

[17] *Lovedale Past and Present: a Record of Two Thousand Names*, Lovedale, Lovedale Press, 1887.

keeper in Port Elizabeth in the late 1860s, and was beginning to feel an urge to be educated. The account continues:

> He came to Lovedale in 1871, and his case is one of the most remarkable results of Lovedale work. A stray leaf of the *Isigidimi Sama-Xosa*, which he picked up and read during his dinner hour at Port Elizabeth, was the first cause of his attention being drawn to the place. On enquiry he found it was 150 miles distant, and he then resolved to walk it and seek admission.[18]

No one among the Ngoni when William Koyi first arrived in Malawi could read, and certainly, no one would have heard of the newspaper *Isigidimi sama Xosa*. But it is at least possible that, as Koyi gathered a small group of young men around him, and talked to them (as we know he did) about his own life, he may have shared with them the story of how he first heard about Lovedale. In that way the name of the newspaper may have become associated with William Koyi himself, and, eventually found its way into the later song.[19]

It is also very possible that, Koyi's friends at Lovedale would have sent him copies of *Isigidimi sama Xosa* and that he may have shown them to his early pupils the Tembo brothers, once they had learnt how to read.

But yet another possibility intrigues me. It is possible that when Koyi first came among the Ngoni they asked him, 'Who are you? What are you doing here? To which he may well have replied, 'I am a messenger: isigidimi.' This might then be interpreted either as a messenger of the *wazungu*, or, as a messenger of God. In practice, of course, Koyi was both. The most common historical meaning of the word in Xhosa, Koyi's own language, is 'one who brings news from the king'. In a religious sense, he may have seen this as the best way of explaining his role as a Christian missionary.

The word ***isigidimi*** appears several times in the Old Testament section of the Zulu Bible published in 1879. It is always used to mean a human messenger, rather than an angel. Whatever the explanation of the name *isigidimi* as it has been applied to William Koyi, the fact that (in its Tumbuka form *sigidini*) it still exists more than one hundred and twenty years after he died is a testimony to the enduring affection in which William Koyi is held by the people of northern Malawi.

---

[18] *Ibid.,* 125.

[19] The fact that the term 'Nyasalandi' appears in the song probably indicates that it was composed well after Koyi's death, for the term was only adopted (at least by the colonial authorities) in 1907.

Donald Fraser and the Ngoni Church[1]

Introduction

One hundred years ago Malawi was in the grip of famine. In May 1902 *inkosi* Mzukuzuku called together his people to discuss the possibility of migrating from their home near Hora mountain, to a new site further south. One consequence of the decision to move was that the Ngoni asked Donald Fraser— then the missionary in charge of Hora station—to move with them.[2] This in itself was significant. Rather than the Scottish missionaries deciding to open a new station at a place of *their* choosing, the Ngoni invited them to accompany the migration to the area in which we now sit. Indeed, some of the other missionaries, notably Elmslie, were against the mission moving at all, and wanted it to stay at Hora.[3]

I begin in this way, because I think in many ways the incident represents the relationship between Fraser and the Ngoni—a relationship in which he, more than almost any other Scottish missionary, was willing to take seriously the ideas and wishes of the Ngoni people amongst whom he was working.

Donald Fraser arrived in Malawi at the end of 1896, and was posted first to Ekwendeni, where he worked until 1900, when he returned to Scotland on leave. On coming back to Malawi in 1901 he was posted to Hora, where he worked briefly before moving south with Mzukuzuku's Ngoni in 1902. For the rest of his missionary career, until he finally returned to Scotland in 1925, he was based at Embangweni. During these years he developed many policies and practices which were distinct to the Ngoni church in this part of Malawi, and some of which were looked upon with suspicion by some of his more conservative Scottish colleagues. In this lecture I want to highlight several areas of Fraser's relations with the Ngoni, and to try to make the point that the genuinely African church which was created in Mzimba district in the first twenty-five years of the twentieth century, was made possible precisely because Fraser was willing to listen to his Ngoni colleagues, and to encourage at least some aspects of African culture, rather than imposing an entirely European form of Christianity on them.

---

[1] This lecture was delivered at Embangweni on 2nd November 2002, as part of the centenary celebrations of Loudon Mission.

[2] Fraser, *Winning a Primitive People*, 202.

[3] Elmslie to Laws, 2 February 1906, Elmslie File, NLS.

Fraser's Sacramental Conventions

First, let us turn to Fraser's use of huge sacramental conventions, to celebrate baptism and the Lord's Supper. Fraser based his idea for the conventions on the old Scottish highland tradition of the communion season. This was a tradition with which he was very familiar, for his father was well known as a leader of such services all over Argyllshire, and even beyond.[4] It is very likely that Fraser had attended many such gatherings as a youth, and that this experience helped to produce the sacramental conventions in *uNgoni*.

Yet there were many differences, too, between the gatherings held by Fraser, and those of the Scottish highlands. In the first place, Fraser included baptism, as well as communion, as an integral part of his conventions—a tradition which was practically unknown in the highlands. Secondly, although the highland seasons, lasting as they did for about five days, obviously included a good deal of teaching, this was mainly designed as a preparation for the sacrament of communion. In Fraser's gatherings the teaching was based much more on the Keswick convention pattern, and aimed at 'the deepening of Christian life'.[5] Finally, there was a very significant theological difference in the approach of church members to the sacrament of communion. In the highland tradition the sacrament was preceded by a sermon known as 'fencing the table' which warned possible communicants of the dangers of partaking unworthily. In Scotland, often only a small percentage of those eligible actually took part in the sacrament. In the conventions in *uNgoni* the emphasis was much more on the joy of the occasion, with every possible church member eager to take part.

The first of these conventions was held at Ekwendeni in May 1898, when people travelled from many parts of *uNgoni* to be present. The first group of these visitors, about seventy from Mpherembe's district, began arriving on the Monday, bringing with them a sheep and a goat to help provide food.[6] To accommodate such groups temporary huts (*misasa*) were erected all around Ekwendeni. A special open-air platform, surrounded by a large grass enclosure, was also constructed, in which to hold the main services.[7] These began on Wednesday, with meetings several times a day. In the afternoons the Ngoni teachers held meetings in six of the surrounding villages. In the evenings the teachers held informal services around Ekwendeni, and Fraser, Stuart and Henderson (on a visit from Khondowe) held further meetings for

---

[4] *Free Church of Scotland Monthly*, February 1893, 43.

[5] *The Aurora*, Vol. 3, June 1899, 19.

[6] Elmslie, *Among the Wild Ngoni*, 308-09.

[7] Fraser, *Autobiogrpahy of an African*, 140.

prayer and study with the Ngoni church leaders. The climax of the convention was the baptism of 195 adults and 89 children, and the communion service in which 365 Christians took part, but at which the congregation is said to have numbered nearly 4000. A final service was held later on Sunday during which an appeal was made for volunteers to go and teach the Senga in the Marambo in what is now eastern Zambia. According to Fraser many responded.[8]

The following year the convention was even bigger. An estimated 6600 were present at some of the services, and between two and three thousand were said to have come from a distance. 309 adults and 148 children were baptised, and 672 people took communion.[9] Most of the leading missionaries were present for this second convention. Dr. and Mrs. Laws had travelled from Khondowe with Miss McCallum; so too had Dr. and Mrs. Elmslie, just back from furlough. Rev. MacAlpine came up from Bandawe.

Laws and others wrote home to Scotland in glowing terms of what had taken place,[10] and, on the surface, nothing may have seemed to epitomise more clearly the new way of life which appeared to be replacing traditional Ngoni values. There is evidence to suggest, however, that, far from being an alien importation, the sacramental convention initiated by Fraser was successful for precisely the opposite reason—that it reminded the Ngoni of one of the most important of traditional African festivals—the Nguni feast of the first fruits—the *incwala*.

First of all it is clear that for as long as fourteen years before the arrival of Fraser in *uNgoni*, and indeed, well before the first Ngoni converts were baptised, some Ngoni villages were already making use of Christian worship to fulfil a need in their own religious observance apparently left by the disappearance of the *incwala*. As early as December 1882 M'mbelwa had asked William Koyi to hold a special service to pray for good crops. Though mission work among the Ngoni was still in its infancy, and the first Ngoni converts were not to be baptised for another eight years, 1500 people attended the service which Koyi held—a clear indication of its importance in the eyes of the Ngoni.[11] By the late 1880s services of thanksgiving before harvesting the crops were being held regularly in some of the villages. In

---

[8] The main accounts of the convention are in Elmslie, *Wild Ngoni*, 306-16, Fraser, *Autobiography*, 140-45, Fraser, *Primitive People*, 92-93, and *Free Church of Scotland Monthly*, September 1898.

[9] Fraser to Smith, , 7 June 1899, Ms. 7882, NLS.

[10] *Free Church of Scotland Monthly*, September 1899, and *The Aurora,* Vol. 3, June 1899, 'Impressions of a Visitor'.

[11] Koyi to Laws, 19 January 1883, Shepperson collection, Edinburgh University Library.

May 1888 the people of Chinyera asked George Williams (the last of the Xhosa missionaries from Lovedale) to hold such a service. The attendance was around four hundred, as opposed to an average of around fifty at the weekly services in the period immediately preceding.[12] In May 1889 Elmslie wrote to Laws that thanksgiving services were 'taking the place of the first-fruits feasts in the villages'.[13] In his book *Among the Wild Ngoni* Elmslie makes it clear that the demand for such services had come 'on the people's initiative'.[14] The practice obviously was meaningful to the Ngoni, for the following year, when Elmslie was on furlough, several villages in the Njuyu area approached the Scottish missionary Charles Stuart and asked him to hold a thanksgiving service. There is a further reference to the practice in 1891.[15] The missionaries interpreted these requests as a rejection of the old ways in favour of the new. In fact, a more accurate interpretation would seem to be that the Ngoni were adapting Christianity to their own religious needs. Thus, while the sacramental conventions were to a large extent new in their scope and content, they were also, at the same time, seen by the Ngoni to be a continuation of existing mission practice, as well as of an established Ngoni initiative.

Fraser's conventions had a wider significance. They involved the assembling together at the mission station of large companies of people from all over *uNgoni*, just as in the old days they would have come to the chief's kraal for the *incwala* ceremony. The length of the ceremonies was approximately the same, and in the same way whole families came, carrying their cooking utensils and their food. Compare, for example the following two descriptions, the first by A.T. Bryant in his book *The Zulu People* of the traditional first fruits feast, the second referring to the sacramental conventions among the Ngoni.

> Every man, every young bride, every carrier-boy, and every girl, wended their way together to the regimental headquarters of their particular male folk, the boys carrying the sleeping-mats and karosses of their fathers and elder brothers, the girls a food supply for at least a week.

> By Tuesday evening the footpaths were full. Whole families were coming, the mothers and daughters carrying cooking-pots on their heads and bags of flour,

[12] George Williams, 'Report on Tshinyera', no date, [around October 1888], Ms. 7891, NLS.

[13] Elmslie to Laws, 17 May 1889

[14] Elmslie, *Wild Ngoni*, 185.

[15] Stuart to Laws, 7 June 1890, and *FCSM*, September 1891, 269.

the men with strings of maize cobs on their shoulders and other produce of their gardens for the collection, and often a tired child on their backs.[16]

The two accounts are remarkably similar, and Fraser was aware of some, at least, of the similarities. It is doubtful if he had anything more than the vaguest outline of what was involved in the *incwala* but he did know about the national gatherings of the Ngoni which welded together the nation and often preceded war raids, and in one of his accounts of the early conventions he made the connection clear.

> In the olden days the unity of the tribe used to be expressed in the national gatherings for raiding. Such meetings could no longer be held. Now the unity of the tribe was to be expressed in the national Christian Conventions.[17]

If Fraser was aware of a national significance in the event, it is likely that many of the Ngoni would have noticed it also.

A further similarity between the *incwala* and the conventions was in the practice of constructing *misasa* (temporary grass huts). Though in some ways the building of such huts was nothing out of the ordinary, it was precisely because of this that the construction was important. Most buildings and ceremonies connected with a Christian mission a hundred years ago were extraordinary from the African point of view. They were strange and foreign. The building of *misasa* and indeed, many of the other details of the conventions, were important for their very 'Africanness'; they allowed people to feel at home.

The second point is much more specific. The *misasa* of an *incwala* ceremony had two quite distinct functions. First, they served as temporary huts for the visiting regiments; but secondly the most sacred part of the ceremony— the taking of medicine by the king to strengthen both him and the whole tribe—took place inside a specially constructed grass shelter.[18] At the sacramental convention grass shelters were used both as houses, and as a large open-air enclosure in which the congregation gathered to receive the sacraments.

Finally, the first sacramental convention in 1898 took place at the time of the full moon - the very time when the traditional *incwala* feast reached its climax.[19]

---

[16] Bryant, *Zulu People*, 515; Elmslie, *Wild Ngoni*, 309.

[17] Fraser, *Autobiography*, 142-43.

[18] See, for example, Hilda Kuper, *An African Aristocracy*, 215; and A.T. Bryant, *Zulu People*, 516.

[19] Elmslie, *Wild Ngoni*, 312.

Fraser was not deliberately creating a Christianized *incwala;* but what is likely is that there were enough similarities in the traditional and Christian celebrations for the conventions to strike a note of responsiveness in the Ngoni who attended them. Another indication of the response and enthusiasm are the numbers attending the conventions in relation to those directly involved in the sacraments. In 1898 the attendance was four thousand, though only 365 of those were church members who could partake of communion. The following year the relevant numbers were 6600 and 672; once again, ten times as many people attended the convention as were able to take communion. The sacramental conventions begun by Fraser, and adopted so enthusiastically by the Ngoni, continued well into the twentieth century. What is certainly evident is that the various factors which helped to give the conventions their distinctive character together contributed powerfully to the growth of Christianity among the Ngoni.

Ngoni Christian Music

Another distinctive feature of Fraser's work which was closely connected with his conventions was his encouragement of the composition by Ngoni Christians of indigenous church music. Singing competitions were often held during the annual conventions, and up to fifty new hymns might be heard in the course of one convention.[20] Though closely connected with Fraser, Ngoni composition of Christian hymns was not started by him, but pre-dated his arrival in *uNgoni.* Furthermore it took its strength not simply from missionary encouragement, but from the inherent Ngoni love of music and strong tradition of composition.

This tradition is reflected in the Ngoni songs collected by the anthropologist Margaret Read during her field-work in Mzimba district in the 1930s.[21] While some of these songs were comparatively modern, others went back to the time of Zwangendaba. The growing integration of Christianity with Ngoni life is shown in this instance by two quite specific connections between traditional Ngoni music and Christian worship. In the first place, as Margaret Read discovered, Ngoni Christian ministers used some of these traditional songs as sermon illustrations, to highlight such things as the difficulties of polygamy.[22] In the second place, some at least of the hymns

---

[20] *United Free Church of Scotland Missionary Record (UFCSMR),* March 1902, 118-19; and April 1903, 165-66.
[21] 'Ngoni Songs', Read Papers, I/10, London School of Economics; and Margaret Read, 'Songs of the Ngoni People', in *Bantu Studies,* 11(1), 1937.
[22] Read, 'Songs', 7.

composed by Ngoni Christians were set to traditional tunes, as, for example, the well known hymn *Wakuchema, wakuchema vyaru vyose* [He is calling, He is calling all countries] which is said to have been composed to the tune with which chief's messenger traditionally called the people together into the kraal.[23]

First Ngoni contacts with Christian music were with Zulu or Xhosa hymns introduced from South Africa by William Koyi in the early 1880s.[24] By 1886 Elmslie had produced the small booklet *Izongoma zo Mlungu*— almost certainly the first printed book in *siNgoni*—which as well as the ten commandments, the Lord's Prayer and a few selected scripture passages, also contained Elmslie's translations of fourteen hymns, including 'Just as I am', 'Hallelujah what a Saviour' and 'O Come all ye Faithful'.[25] Four years later Elmslie wrote to Laws that he had obtained permission from missionaries to the Zulu to use their hymns in *uNgoni*.[26]

By then, however, Livingstonia Christians in the different areas of the mission's work were already beginning to compose their own hymns. Almost certainly the earliest of these was not a Ngoni example, but was one by Albert Namalambe (the first convert of the Livingstonia mission) probably composed in the early 1880s,[27] which was revived in 1975 for the Livingstonia centenary celebrations. Amongst the Tonga also a similar development was taking place, and MacAlpine singled out Samuel Kauti Longwe as the outstanding contributor.[28]

It was primarily among the Ngoni, however, that the tradition of hymn composition developed. It was already well under way when Fraser arrived in *uNgoni*, and was particularly strong at Njuyu station, at that time under the control of Mawelera Tembo. Both Fraser and Stuart commented in 1897, on the value of these local compositions, which were used, not only in worship, but also in school instruction.[29] It is significant that this tradition developed in an area so strongly influenced by Mawelera Tembo, for he was not only one of the leading Ngoni composers of Christian music, but remained right up until his death an expert on traditional Ngoni songs.

---

[23] Helen Taylor, personal interview, 16 January 1974.

[24] *FCSM*, August 1883, 241 – letter from William Koyi dated February 1883.

[25] W.A. Elmslie, *Izongoma zo Mlungu* , Blantyre, 1886.

[26] Elmslie to Laws, 4 September 1890, Ms. 7894, NLS

[27] 'Albert's Hymn', Livingstonia Papers, Box 4, National Archives of Malawi (NAM).

[28] 'Lectures on African Colleagues', Macalpine Papers, Special Collections, Edinburgh University Library.

[29] *The Aurora*, Vol. 1, June 1897, 22; and *FCSM*, July 1897, 97.

Fraser, then, found an already thriving tradition of Ngoni Christian music by the time he arrived in *uNgoni* at the beginning of 1897. His contribution was to encourage and organise this tradition to an extent totally unmatched in any other area of Livingstonia's work. Soon after his return from Scotland in 1901 he was already organising musical competitions between the different schools. At Hora in 1901 about two dozen new hymns were heard; the following year fifty new compositions were submitted, and Fraser commented, 'Some pieces were particularly beautiful, and it was felt that a valuable contribution had been made to the hymnology of the Central African Church'.[30]

By the time that the new church at Loudon was opened in 1904, the musical festival had become an annual event, closely linked with the sacramental conventions. It is clear that Ngoni hymns were becoming part of the ethos of the conventions, and of Ngoni Christian life, in a way which obviously differed from other parts of Malawi where the mission was working. Writing of her visit to the Hora convention in 1902, Miss Martin, a missionary at Khondowe, described how she sat on a hill and watched groups of people wending their way towards the mission station, singing as they came:

> The singing still went on, and I noticed, as they stood to go through one stanza, that not only were the people clapping their hands, but were also at times accompanying the singing with slow movements of the body and the elevation of their sticks. I was quite at a loss to understand what it all meant.[31]

Though new missionaries, or those from outside *uNgoni*, may have found it difficult to understand or appreciate the mixture of the old and the new which this musical blossoming represented, Fraser had no such difficulties. He recognised that the inherent Ngoni love of music was best encouraged as a channel through which the newly emerging Christian faith might be expressed and shared.

When in 1910, a new Tumbuka hymnbook was being drawn up for use throughout the Livingstonia mission area, Fraser's membership of the committee ensured the inclusion of many Ngoni hymns. To-day, in *Sumu za Ukristu,* 127 out of 401 hymns included are attributed to Malawian writers. In fact this is certainly an underestimation, since many unattributed hymns are also of African composition - notable among them number 46, '*Hena mwana mberere*' [Behold the Lamb of God] one of Charles Chinula's best-known hymns. Of the twenty-four African writers named, twenty-one are from *uNgoni*. Among the Ngoni writers included, the most prolific are Peter

---

[30] *UFCSMR*, March 1902, 118-19; and April 1903, 165-66.

[31] *UFCSMR*, March 1902, 166.

Thole, Charles Chinula, Mawelera Tembo, Jonathan Chirwa, Hezekiah Tweya and Elija Chavula.

Several Ngoni hymns are also included in the hymnbook of the Blantyre synod of the Church of Central Africa, Presbyterian, and in various English anthologies of Africa hymns published in Britain and the United States. The most recent of these international compilations, *Come Let Us Walk This Road Together*, edited by Tom Colvin, was published in USA in 1997, and contains English translations of hymns by Mawelera Tembo, Peter Thole, Ben Nhlane, Charles Chinula, Elijah Chavura, Thomas Ngoma and Yesaya Ngulube. [32]

The existence of a strong Ngoni tradition of musical composition, its adaptation by the Ngoni to Christian hymnology, and Fraser's sympathetic encouragement of this trend, all helped to integrate Christianity into the mainstream of Ngoni life, and to some extent helped to preserve the Ngoni language as a medium of ritual and worship.

Masessioni ghachoko and Balalakazi4

In many ways Fraser stepped out of line with his Scottish colleagues, in order to encourage greater local participation in the church. Two examples of this were in his use of sub-sessions (*Masessioni ghachoko*) and women elders (*balalakazi*). The system of sub-sessions began in 1908, shortly after Fraser's return from furlough in Scotland, and at the beginning of an unbroken stretch of five years at Loudon. The huge Loudon district was divided into a dozen large parishes. Each one was put under the control of an evangelist and a few elders and deacons, who formed a sub-session, with responsibility for the day-to-day running of the church in their area. At the end of 1908 Fraser reported that the system was working admirably, and had led to better pastoral care, a more careful administration of discipline, and a great increase in the liberality of the people. [33]

Although their powers were limited, the sub-sessions fulfilled a useful and important function. They had power to hear cases, and could suspend and restore hearers and catechumens. Cases involving church members, however, had to be referred to the main session at Loudon. [34] Even in such cases, however, the sub-session could investigate the details of the dispute and present them to the Loudon session, so that a more accurate decision could be reached. In addition to the hearing of cases, the sub-sessions were

---

[32] Tom Colvin (Editor and Translator), *Come Let Us Walk This Road Together*, 1997.

[33] *Livingstonia Annual Reports for 1908,* 'Report for Loudon', 27.

[34] Session Minute Book – Middle Rukuru (Mariba), 14 November 1916, NAM.

responsible for the day-to-day running of the congregation, the organisation of financial contributions, and the pastoral supervision of the Christians in the area. They met regularly and kept minutes which were occasionally checked either by a missionary, or, increasingly after 1914, by an African minister such as Jonathan Chirwa.[35]

They appear also to have been used as a means of ascertaining grass-roots opinion on important matters. For example, in 1913, after the introduction of the barrier act, both the questions of the introduction of a central fund to support African ministers, and of a proposed creed for the church, were sent down to Loudon session. They proposed that both documents should be translated into chiTumbuka and sent down to the sub-sessions for further discussion.[36] One result of such detailed discussion was that while most sessions agreed to the setting up of a central fund, Loudon reported that they thought it was too early for such a move.[37]

In spite of their limited powers, it would appear that sub-sessions were both popular and useful. They probably developed out of the more modest deacons' courts, and were merely the institutionalizing by Fraser of a grass-roots control of the local church which was already in existence anyway. Nevertheless they were one of the very few church bodies which met at that period without the presence and control of European missionaries, and as such, their importance should not be underestimated.

Another distinct grouping organised by Fraser during this period were the *balalakazi* [women elders]. They were first elected in 1901 at Hora to provide for the spiritual oversight of the female Christians.[38] In the same year, Fraser proposed in presbytery the organisation and training of an order of deaconesses; but no decision was taken.[39] At Loudon during this intervening period the *balalakazi* occupied something of an intermediate position between elders and deacons. During communion, for example, they sat on the platform with the other elders, but did not distribute the elements.[40] Though the eligibility of women as deacons was accepted by presbytery in 1922, it was not until 1935, and a strong appeal by Fraser's widow Dr. Agnes Fraser, that presbytery agreed to recognise women as elders on the same basis as men.[41]

[35] *Ibid.*, various entries, 1914.
[36] Loudon Session Minute book, 13 February 1913, NAM.
[37] North Livingstonia Presbytery Minutes, 20 August 1913, NAM.
[38] *Livingstonia Annual Report 1901*, 'Report for Hora', 16.
[39] North Livingstonia Presbytery Minutes, 27 May 1901, NAM
[40] Agnes Fraser, *Donald Fraser of Livingstonia*, 89.
[41] North Livingstonia Presbytery Minutes, 20 July 1922, and 6 July 1935, NAM.

Several factors contributed to the long delay in recognising women elders. First while the place of women in the non-Ngoni societies of northern Malawi was of considerable importance in socio-economic terms, they were allowed very little political power by their male counterparts. Secondly, even in Ngoni society, where the royal women, at least, had considerable political power, this was normally exercised as a distinct female group, rather than in a mixed group of men and women. Thus the idea of *balalakazi,* while more acceptable to the Ngoni than to other groups, took the form even here of a separate office. Thirdly, the ecclesiastical and social background of the Scottish missionaries themselves did not encourage the recognition of female elders. Indeed, it was not until 1966, thirty years after the church in Livingstonia had taken the step, and more than sixty years after Fraser had first introduced *balalakazi* in *uNgoni,* that women became eligible for election as elders in the Church of Scotland.

To the extent that Fraser's scheme was not adopted by presbytery in the early years of the century, and therefore was not officially recognised by the church, it may be said to have failed. Agnes Fraser believed the scheme failed because it was premature.[42] Yet Margaret Read compares the groupings of men and women elders in *uNgoni* to the *madoda* and *manina* groupings of traditional Ngoni society,[43] and there can be little doubt that the continuing *de facto* existence of the *balalakazi* in *uNgoni* did much to strengthen the church, especially with the increasing drain of male leadership due to the growing necessity of migrant labour.

Fraser and Ngoni Culture

Fraser's attitude to Ngoni culture in general was, on the whole, much more positive than that of most of his colleagues. The anthropologist Margaret Read, in writing of the Dutch Reformed missionaries among Gomani's Ngoni, commented on 'their lack of interest in Ngoni culture as contrasted with the Scottish mission's tolerance and respect for certain elements'.[44] While this comparison is clearly true, it might be more accurate to say that a distinctive Ngoni culture was much stronger in the north, and therefore the missionaries had to come to terms with it in one way or another. This is not to say that the Livingstonia missionaries were universally sympathetic to Ngoni culture—far less that the Ngoni were always satisfied with missionary

---

[42] Agnes Fraser, 'A Missionary's Wife among African Women', *International Review of Missions*, Vol. 3, July 1914, 461.

[43] 'The Ngoni and Adjustments to Social Change', unpublished typescript, Read Papers, LSE.

[44] *Ibid.*

attitudes. They were not. Furthermore, the Scottish missionaries, Fraser included, made no attempt to accept Ngoni culture as a whole, but judged individual aspects of it against their own standards of right and wrong, or sometimes against similar customs in surrounding tribes. Nevertheless, given these provisos, it is probably true to say that the Scottish missionaries in general, and Fraser in particular, had a more sympathetic attitude to Ngoni culture than that displayed by missionaries to other Ngoni groups elsewhere in Malawi.

Fraser's general attitude to African culture may best he summed up in one quotation from an article he wrote towards the end of his career, and which was based on a lecture which he gave to more than two hundred delegates concerned with Christian mission in Africa at the Le Zoute conference in Belgium in 1926:

> I fear the evangel which de-nationalizes, which refuses to recognize the power of the Gospel to purify what is not essentially wrong, and which preaches first through prohibitions, rather than by the attraction of what is positive... [W]e come not to destroy distinctive nationality, but to fulfil what men have searched after gropingly; and for the enrichment of the world to retain and purify all that is not evil. Society has been safeguarded by many a social and magical tie, and none of these should be cut unless we give in their place surer bonds... If we only denounce magic we leave society unprotected and unguided. [45]

Yet the difficulty of a European missionary of Fraser's generation reaching an accommodation with Ngoni culture which was totally acceptable to Ngoni Christians themselves, can be seen in the reaction of Charles Chinula towards Fraser's attitude to traditional dancing. Fraser strictly distinguished between those dances which he considered immoral and those which were acceptable. Of the latter, the main dance of which he approved was the *ingoma,* though even here he sometimes felt that it took up too much time. Nevertheless he approved of it, and even arranged a special session of many traditional dances for W.P. Livingstone, the missionary biographer, and editor of the *Missionary Record,* when he visited Loudon.[46] In spite of what appeared to his European colleagues as a liberal attitude to dancing, Fraser's outlook did not satisfy Charles Chinula, who, while a teacher at Loudon in

---

[45] Fraser, 'The Evangelistic Approach to the African', in *International Review of Missions,* Vol. XV, 1926, 438-49.
[46] W.P. Livingstone, 'In the Bush with Donald Fraser', in *Life and Work,* January 1934, 18-19.

1908, encouraged his pupils to take part in secret dance sessions at the school.[47]

Nevertheless Fraser's attitude to Ngoni culture was basically sympathetic. While opposed to individual elements within the culture, such as polygamy and beer-drinking, he was, at the same time, highly attracted to the Ngoni as a people. While he was opposed to some forms of traditional medicine (notably the *kayeyi* practitioners who entered *uNgoni* in 1902 selling medicine which was claimed could ward off both curses and death)[48] he also recognised that many local herbal medicines were effective, and even made use of them himself to treat some sick calves.[49]

On occasions Fraser's attitudes to African culture could bring him into conflict with his missionary colleagues. One such occasion was the discussion in Presbytery in October 1911 of the issue of *chokoro*—marriage to a deceased brother's widow. This topic had already been discussed three times in Presbytery. As a result of these discussions the ruling of Presbytery was 'that a man may not marry the widow of his deceased brother'.[50] This ruling, however, was apparently not acceptable to many Christians in *uNgoni*, and in October 1911 Loudon session brought up the question again. MacAlpine, seconded by Walter Henderson, the builder, moved that 'as this matter was discussed on two previous occasions...the Presbytery do not re-open the question'.[51] Fraser pressed ahead, however, moving an amendment, seconded by Edward Bothi Manda, that

> Considering that marriage with a deceased brother's wife is common native custom, and is not clearly contrary to Biblical Law, the Presbytery, while discouraging the custom, do not think such a marriage sufficient cause for discipline.[52]

This amendment was carried by nineteen votes to nine. The following year, however, while Fraser was on leave in Scotland, Elmslie and Laws combined to reverse Fraser's motion.[53] Their proposal was passed unanimously—probably because *chokoro* had been declared illegal by the colonial government. The incident, nevertheless shows very clearly the way in which Fraser was prepared to take the side of the African church, against the opinion of his senior Scottish colleagues Laws, Elmslie and MacAlpine.

---

[47] Quoted in John McCracken, *Politics and Christianity in Malawi*, 196.

[48] *UFCSMR*, October 1902, 450; and Fraser, *Primitive People*, 198-99.

[49] *Ibid.*, 141.

[50] North Livingstonia Presbytery Minutes, 6 November 1907, NAM.

[51] *Ibid.*, 20 October 1911.

[52] *Ibid.*

[53] *Ibid.*, 18 October 1912.

Above all, while by no means entirely satisfactory to all Ngoni Christians, Fraser's attitudes were sufficiently open to encourage the Ngoni to work out their own response to Christianity in the light of Ngoni culture, and to find an answer which gave to that culture a place of some importance in the new way of life. That the Ngoni were able to preserve a distinctive and valid culture, while turning in large numbers to Christianity, was due mainly to their own inherent strength and cohesion, but partly also to the sympathetic approach of Fraser.

There were also times when Fraser's policies made him temporarily very unpopular among the Ngoni (though this occasion of celebration is perhaps not the time to dwell upon them in any detail). The most obvious occasion was early in the First World War. At a time when *inkosi* Chimtunga was refusing to supply carriers (a refusal which led to his deposition and exile by the British) Fraser was supporting the war and the need to recruit *amtengatenga*. These attitudes led to him becoming temporarily unpopular with many of the Ngoni during the First World War.[54]

Fraser's African Relationships

Yet when all is said and done, Fraser's most important contributions might be thought to have been simply in the friendships and relationships which he made with many Malawians, such as Daniel Nhlane, Jonathan Chirwa and Clements Kadalie. Shortage of time does not allow me to speak in much detail of each of these relationships, so let me mention briefly two incidents involving Daniel Nhlane and Clements Kadalie, and then speak in some more detail of Fraser's relationship with Jonathan Chirwa.

First, one story of many, linking Fraser and Daniel Nhlane: in 1899 a European from Zimbabwe named William Robert Ziehl entered *uNgoni* to buy cattle. While there he committed theft, rape, and murder. Fraser, who was at Ekwendeni at the time, wrote to Daniel Nhlane, and asked him to go and investigate. Nhlane and several companions went to see Ziehl, and in the argument which followed, Ziehl was hit over the head with a *ntonga*. Fraser supported Nhlane's action. Ziehl then fled from the area. The Ngoni were so incensed that Fraser found it difficult to hold them back; so he suggested sending out an *impi* to pursue and arrest Ziehl: an *impi* which Fraser himself volunteered to lead. At the very last minute Cardew, the government agent at Nkhata Bay sent some of his police to pursue Ziehl, and thus was averted by a just few hours, what would have been the unprecedented sight of a Scottish missionary leading out an Ngoni army.

---

[54] See Thompson, *Christianity in Northern Malawi*, 181-86.

When Ziehl was eventually caught and brought to trial, Fraser firmly supported the actions of Daniel Nhlane and his companions in confronting Ziehl, who was found guilty of eight out of nine charges—though he escaped imprisonment, and was merely fined £50. The Ngoni gave Ziehl the nickname *Kanjechi*, which I think might be translated as 'the one who was really beaten into shape'. The incident shows Fraser identifying with and supporting the Ngoni in a time of need. [55]

Next, let us look briefly at one incident involving Fraser and Clements Kadalie. Now immediately, those of you with local knowledge may be asking 'Why is he talking about Clements Kadalie? He was a Tonga; not a Ngoni.' Well that is true; but what is also true is that Clements Kadalie grew up here at Embangweni, where his father was one of the bricklayers working on the building of the church. [56] Kadalie, who was related to both Y.Z. Mwasi and Yakobe Msusa Muwamba, later became internationally famous as the founder of the first major black trade union in South Africa, the Industrial and Commercial Workers' Union.

In 1920, Fraser was on his way home to Scotland, and was passing through Cape Town. There he met both Kadalie, and an unnamed Malawian on his way back from service in Europe during the First World War. When, a few years later, Fraser came to write his last book, *The New Africa*, he chose to begin the book with an account of this meeting, and wrote very positively of the Malawians who had become the trade union leader, and the soldier. Of Kadalie he wrote:

> The Scottish missionary who had taught the Trade Union secretary would possibly have been shocked at the idea of native workmen combining [to go on strike]. But this clever lad had gone on to another school, and other teachers had been educating him since he was a pupil in a mission school. [57]

Clements Kadalie liked Fraser's account of the meeting so much, that when he came to write his own autobiography *My Life and the ICU* he included the whole story, just as Fraser had told it. This account by Fraser shows that his concerns were much wider than the merely religious or spiritual. In writing positively of the trade unionist and the soldier, he was applauding the fact (as he said in the passage) 'that the present generation is stretching out its hands in new demands undreamed of by the fathers'. [58]

---

[55] A more detailed account of this incident can be found in this book in the article, 'Bloodthirsty Savages or Stout-Hearted Zulus?'

[56] Clements Kadalie, *My Life and the ICU*, 31-33.

[57] Fraser, *The New Africa*, 10.

[58] *Ibid.*

Finally, let us look at Fraser's relationship with Jonathan Chirwa, as summed up in his campaign to have Chirwa restored to Christian ministry. Chirwa, following his ordination in 1914, had worked with Fraser at Loudon, before being sent to Mwenzo in 1916 to take charge of the station, and fill the vacancy caused by the death of John Afwenge Banda. While there he committed adultery, and, following a confession to Fraser, resigned his Christian ministry, and was suspended from church membership by the presbytery which met in July 1918 at Khondowe.[59]

Fraser was clerk of Presbytery at the time, and the very personal way in which he worded the minute showed his great affection for Chirwa. In a situation where the minute might normally be cold and formal, Fraser wrote: 'With great sorrow Presbytery heard their beloved brother Jonathan Chirwa make confession of sin and resign his ministry.'[60] For the next six years the Ngoni church, closely supported by Fraser, carried on a constant struggle to have Chirwa restored.

In July 1919 presbytery received various petitions for the restoration of Chirwa to the Christian ministry, and Fraser and Andrew Mkochi reported on his conduct in the previous year. Presbytery decided by twenty-three votes to nine that he should not be restored yet, but Mkochi and Fraser were given permission to appoint him to any work they saw fit.[61] That full restoration did not take place then, only twelve months after Chirwa's suspension, is hardly surprising, but when restoration was again refused the following year, it became obvious that some members of presbytery, including several very influential missionaries, were opposed to restoration in the foreseeable future. Presbytery recorded that

> The fear was expressed by many speakers lest the presbytery seem ahead of Christian public opinion and by a premature restoration lower the estimate of the Christian ministry at the very outset of its history in the country.[62]

Yet it seems clear, that in *uNgoni* at any rate, Christian public opinion favoured restoration, for a Ngoni elder of the period was quite clear that 'people wanted him to come back'.[63] The influence of the European missionaries on presbytery was still very great at this time. Fraser was on leave in Scotland between 1920 and 1923.[64] During his absence no other European

---

[59] Livingstonia Presbytery Minutes, 22 July 1918, NAM.
[60] *Ibid.*
[61] *Ibid.*, 23 July 1919.
[62] *Ibid.*, 20 July 1920.
[63] Rev. Mbalo Mtonga, personal interview, 29 December 1971.
[64] The unusual length of this leave was due to the fact that while at home, Fraser led a major

missionary seemed willing, or able, actively to pursue the case for restoration. Those opposed to restoration adopted the tactic of delay. In 1921 the annual petition from the Loudon group of congregations was presented by Andrew Mkochi. The minute merely recorded that, as Jonathan Chirwa was not present no decision was taken.[65]

By now the divisions on the missionary side were becoming more clear-cut. At the beginning of the year Fraser had written to Elmslie from Scotland, protesting his dissatisfaction that Chirwa had not been restored, and implying that such restoration would be in accordance with the mind of Christ. Elmslie, however, dismissed such a view, claiming that 'Paul's clear actions in an atmosphere such as we have point to caution'. He added:

> I think Jonathan has been pampered since his case came up, and his repentance has made him a hero in the attitude of many. I myself think he should not have been permitted to take any public duties. He was suspended from the ministry which is not merely dispensing the sacraments.[66]

The latter references are to the fact that Chirwa, in accordance with the permission given to Fraser and Mkochi in 1919, had been gradually allowed to assume various ecclesiastical duties in the Loudon area, and was, by now, performing the duties of an evangelist.[67]

Once again, in July 1922, Loudon petitioned presbytery for Chirwa's restoration. This time a special committee was set up to enquire into the case, which reported back four days later that no final decision should be taken until the two European missionaries who had heard the original case— Laws and Fraser—returned from furlough.[68] This effectively postponed the decision until the presbytery of 1924, which met at Khondowe in September of that year.

By that time Fraser had returned from furlough, and became, once again, directly involved in the case. Earlier in the year he had taken Chirwa on *ulendo* with him (helping to dispense communion in the outlying districts around Loudon) and had described him as 'my beloved native helper'.[69] It was clear that the time for a decision had arrived. When presbytery met MacAlpine and Laws proposed that the case be referred to a joint synod of Livingstonia and Blantyre (who were just about to unite to form the Church

---

missionary campaign in Scotland, and then was elected as Moderator of the United Free Church of Scotland.
[65] Livingstonia Presbytery Minutes, 25 July 1921, NAM.
[66] Elmslie to Laws, 28 January 1921, Box 9, Livingstonia Papers, NAM.
[67] Petros H. Moyo, personal interview, 28 December 1971.
[68] Livingstonia Presbytery Minutes, 20 & 24 July 1922.
[69] *UFCSMR*, June 1924, 264.

of Central Africa, Presbyterian). The Ngoni church was by now in no mood for further delays and two leading Ngoni Christians, Andrew Mkochi and Yobe Nhlane proposed 'that the case be proceeded with now'.[70] This proposal in itself was an indication of their determination, for seldom, if ever, up to that point, had African Christians so directly opposed the will of Dr. Laws in Presbytery. Their amendment was, nevertheless, carried by twenty-nine votes to five.[71]

Immediately after that Mkochi moved and Fraser seconded 'that Jonathan Chirwa be now restored'. Laws moved that he be not restored. At this point the minutes merely record that the meeting was adjourned for the night. In fact, the adjournment was necessary because the strong feelings expressed on both sides were getting out of hand.[72] When it reconvened the following morning Laws changed his amendment to 'that Jonathan Chirwa be not restored now', and was seconded by MacAlpine. When a vote was taken, only two voted not to restore, and thirty-six to restore, and Jonathan Chirwa was immediately re-instated as a minister.[73]

Behind the personalities of the 1924 presbytery deeper issues were involved. According to one eyewitness account African opinion was unanimously in favour of restoration, but Laws and MacAlpine refused, arguing 'it is not law in Scotland'.[74] Their argument was that for the purpose of maintaining the high moral standards expected of the clergy, no minister guilty of a serious moral lapse should be restored. This was a view which Fraser had had to fight right since 1918, for when Chirwa had first resigned his ministry and been suspended from church membership, some had argued that he should be deposed with no hope of future reinstatement. At the time Fraser had argued strongly against that line, and now again, in the presbytery of 1924, in answer to the argument that it was not law in Scotland, he countered, 'This is an African church. We cannot take the laws of home.' [75]

Four years later, in 1928, Jonathan Chirwa was elected as moderator of presbytery, and is remembered as one of the finest of the early ministers. By the early 1930s he had become an elder statesman at Loudon, described by one young missionary of the period as 'a real father-in-God to me' and by another as 'a very loving and loveable man'.[76]

---

[70] Livingstonia Presbytery Minutes, 11 September 1924, NAM.

[71] *Ibid.*

[72] Petros H. Moyo, personal interview, 28 December 1971.

[73] Livingstonia Presbytery Minutes, 12 September 1924.

[74] Petros H. Moyo, personal interview, 28 December 1971.

[75] *Ibid.*

[76] Rev. W.H. Watson & Miss Helen Taylor, personal interviews, 8 October 1974 & 16

Conclusion

Even in this long lecture, it has been possible to cover only a small part of all that we might say about Donald Fraser and Loudon. I cannot finish without praising also Dr. Agnes Fraser. One of the things which distinguished Donald Fraser was the large amount of time he spent travelling around Mzimba district on *ulendo*. Sometimes he was away for many weeks at a time. During these periods his wife Agnes was in effective control of the station. She was, of course, also a medical doctor, working at the hospital at Loudon; and after Fraser's death, she returned to Africa to work in Zambia with the United Mission to the Copperbelt. She was a woman of great talent and achievement in her own right.

Donald Fraser died in Scotland in 1933. His remains were cremated, and two years later his widow Agnes brought his ashes back to Loudon to be buried. Today, if we leave this church, and walk just a short distance, we will come to the graveyard where, side by side, are buried the remains of Donald Fraser and Jonathan Chirwa—the Scottish missionary and the African minister. Nothing could speak more elegantly or movingly of the love and respect which Fraser and the Ngoni had for each other. Together, they helped to create a church which was at the same time, both Christian and African. I hope we may agree that this remains the case today.

January 1974.

Making a Road for the Lord: the Centenary of the Opening of the *Gorodi*[1]

Introduction

We are here today, not simply to celebrate a road, but to remember the people who planned it, and built it, and used it; and to think about all the other developments that the road made possible.

Just recently in Edinburgh, where I work, I found an old diary or notebook belonging to Dr. Robert Laws.[2] It was in the Special Collections of Edinburgh university library. Dr. Laws was a very careful man, he did not like to waste anything; so he had used this diary many times. It began in 1873, before he even came to Malawi; then it went on to 1878, three years after he first arrived at Cape Maclear. The entry for 1878 begins:

> On Monday 12th August at 1-40 p.m. we left Livingstonia in the *Ilala* to be landed on the west coast to begin our journey in search of a site for our principal Mission Station.[3]

(Here, of course, when he says 'Livingstonia' he does not mean Mumbwe.[4] He means Cape Maclear, which was the first Livingstonia).

The diary then jumps to 1894. The first entry for 1894 begins:

> At Ekwendeni last week… I arranged with Dr. Elmslie to accompany me on the journey which the Livingstonia committee has instructed me to undertake with the view of finding a suitable site for the proposed Missionary Institution.[5]

The diary then moves on from 1894 to 1905, and mentions the last stages of building the *Gorodi* road.

The Search for a Mission Headquarters

These events are important because they help to set the building of the road in its historical context. When the Livingstonia missionaries first came to

---

[1] This lecture was delivered at Livingstonia on 22nd October 2005, as part of the centenary celebrations of the Gorodi road.

[2] Laws' Diary, Robert Laws Papers, Edinburgh University Library, Special Collections, GEN561/1.

[3] Ibid. There are no page numbers in the diary; only dates.

[4] The plateau now generally known as Livingstonia is called locally 'Mumbwe'. It is also known as 'Khondowe', after a local chief.

[5] Laws' Diary, EUL, Special Collections, GEN 561/1.

Malawi in 1875 they brought with them the steamer *Ilala*. The ship was central to their supply line—the way they got from the east coast of Africa to the Mission. They therefore needed to find a site for the mission which was on or near the lake. This is one of the main reasons why they first settled at Cape Maclear. But Cape Maclear proved to be unhealthy. By early 1881, as W.P. Livingstone reports in *Laws of Livingstonia*, many people in Scotland were beginning to think the mission a failure: five years' work, five graves, one convert![6] And so the search for a new headquarters began, as we have seen in the diary, and Bandawe was chosen. It is important to note, by the way, that Bandawe was not opened in 1881, as some books say. It had actually been opened in 1878 as an experimental station,[7] while most of the missionaries still remained at Cape Maclear; but in 1881 it became the head-quarters of the Mission.

Once again, Bandawe was chosen because it was on the Lake, and could provide a good base from which the *Ilala* could supply goods to the Mission. But while Bandawe proved a better location than Cape Maclear, it was still unhealthy for Europeans in those days, when there was no known cause or cure for malaria; and so, after several years (and again, as the diary tells us) Laws set out again in 1894 (this time with Dr. Elmslie and Yuriah Chirwa) to look for the third headquarters of the mission. And we all know the story of how they eventually ended up here at Mumbwe. What is important to realise, however, is that, after two stations on the lake which had both claimed the lives of several missionaries, the most important issue this time was to find a site which was healthy for the missionaries. And so this place was chosen. But this created a new problem: the removal of the mission from its main line of supply (the Lake) up into a remote and hard to reach plateau in the interior, raised the question of how supplies were to be transported from the lakeshore to the plateau.

Difficulties and Solutions

At first porters were used to carry goods up the escarpment, but, as those of us who have walked up from the lake know very well, this is very hard work, even without heavy loads on our backs or heads, and soon porters were beginning to complain. We are not here talking merely of carrying bales of cloth, or bags of sugar, which one man could carry on his back, but of very heavy loads such as church organs or printing presses, which in some cases

---

[6] *Laws of Livingstonia*, 184.

[7] The original daily journal from Bandawe, dating back to 1878 is in the National Library of Scotland, Edinburgh, Livingstonia Papers, Mss. 7910-11.

had to be mounted on sledges and dragged up the escarpment by huge teams of men.[8] Imagine trying to drag very heavy equipment up without a road! It became so difficult that sometimes porters refused to work. On one occasion (and here I must apologise to the General Secretary and my other Tonga friends) Laws reported 'the Tonga finally deserted, but the Ngoni carried on'.[9] Even when double wages were offered, it was sometimes difficult to find enough porters to drag supplies up the escarpment.[10]

It was against this background that Laws began to think of building what at first was called a 'wagon road' – a road from the lake to the plateau which could be used by ox carts. And again, we are not talking about the kind of ox carts we know even today in Malawi – pulled by one or two oxen – but of much larger carts pulled by six or eight oxen.[11] This was all the more necessary because Laws had big plans in his head for the development of Livingstonia.

I have in my possession a plan of the plateau, draw by Robert Laws himself, signed, and dated 1899.[12] This was before he went home to Scotland on leave. This does not show the plateau as it was in 1899. It shows the plateau as Robert Laws saw it in his head: as he planned to develop it. It is practically identical to the way it is today. He had plans for what is now the secondary school, the technical school, the dormitories, the Homestead, the church, many houses etc.

In particular, he had plans for several very specific developments which were to take place at the same time as the building of the road. We need to look at these first, to understand why it was so important to build such a road. One fact to begin with: at this period, more than 300 tons of supplies and equipment were sent out to Livingstonia from Britain, and had to be taken from the Lakeshore up to the plateau.

In 1900, while he was back in Scotland on leave, Laws appealed for money to undertake several big projects. These included the water supply, the electricity system, and the telegraph line (as well as the road). Let us look at each of these briefly.

---

[8] See the photograph opposite p. 208 of *Laws of Livingstonia*.
[9] Notes accompanying magic lantern slide set 'Laws of Livingstonia', Centre for the Study of Christianity in the Non-Western World, University of Edinburgh.
[10] Ibid.
[11] See the second photograph on p. 208 of *Laws of Livingstonia*.
[12] A version of this plan appears opposite p. 209 in *Laws of Livingstonia*.

Water, Telegraph and Electricity Schemes

First was the scheme to bring fresh, clean piped water from Nyamkhowa down into the valley at Vunguvungu, and then up again to the plateau. The estimated cost of this was £4000.[13] (In to-day's money that might be around MK50 million). It was paid for by Lord Overtoun – the main financial backer of the mission. In honour of him Laws named the whole enterprise at Livingstonia 'The Overtoun Institution'.

Laws had calculated that the pressure of the water in the pipes as it came down to Vunguvungu and then up to the plateau would be twice as much as the pressure in the water system of Glasgow; so he ordered very strong pipes: 2 and 4 inch diameter steel pipes from Glasgow.[14] These arrived at Chitimba in 1901, and were brought up the escarpment as the road was being built. It took several years to complete the scheme. Eventually, on 20th January 1904, Mrs. Laws switched on the new water system[15] and basically this is the same system which has been serving Livingstonia now for the last one hundred years.

Later in 1904 a second interesting development took place. This was the completion of the telegraph line from the Stone House down to the lakeshore at Chitimba, where it joined the famous Cape to Cairo telegraph system.[16] The completion of the Livingstonia telegraph link meant that messages which had previously taken several months to send by post from Malawi to Scotland could now be sent by telegram in a few hours. Of course one result of this was that Scotland could keep a closer control on Dr. Laws, who previously would start projects before word could come from Scotland telling him to stop!

Laws third project was an electricity system. This would be run by turbines supplying hydroelectric power from the Manchewe river, near the falls. Laws idea was that the electric power would serve two major purposes. It would power the many machines which he was hoping to introduce at Livingstonia, such as the sawmill, the flourmill, the printing press, etc. In addition, however, it would provide electric light for the various departments at the station, especially the schools.

In order to learn more about electricity while he was back in Scotland in 1900, Laws decided to go back to College. He enrolled for classes in electrical engineering at what is now Heriot-Watt university in Edinburgh.

---

[13] *Laws of Livingstonia*, 297.

[14] *Ibid.*, 305.

[15] *United Free Church of Scotland Monthly Record*, March 1904, 115.

[16] *Ibid.*, April 1905, 172, letter from Laws to Fairley Daly, dated 16th December 1904.

At this time Laws was fifty years old, so most of his fellow students were young enough to be his own children.

While I was researching material for this lecture, I managed to find the very notebooks which Laws used to take his notes more than one hundred years ago.[17] He has recorded some of his own experiments in his own neat handwriting. Among these experiments were 'How to calibrate an ammeter', 'Calibrations of a voltmeter', 'To plot the characteristic curve of a dynamo running on an open circuit'. I don't know what all these things mean, but they show the determination of a man willing to learn something new, if it would help develop Livingstonia.

Once again, as with his other projects, Laws had to raise the money in Scotland to pay for the electrical system. He felt it would be particularly useful in the schools. He described how 'After dark, boys could be seen standing outside the evening school, preparing their lessons for the next day by the light [from oil lamps] streaming out of the windows.'[18] Once electric light was available the students of both the day and night schools would be able to study in good conditions.

The electric lights were finally switched on on the evening of 12th October 1905 – the exact thirtieth anniversary of the day when the *Ilala* had first sailed into Lake Malawi, and today, almost exactly one hundred years ago. We have an exact account of the moment the lights were switched on:

> In the evening our native friends, as well as the Europeans, met in the school-church [this, by the way was not the present church, which had not yet been built; it was the original church which was on the road which now runs between the hospital and the doctor's house] which, while the audience assembled was illuminated with two or three of the ordinary good oil-lamps. When all were gathered these lamps were put out, leaving a solitary candle on a table, beside which sat Mrs. Innes, with little James on her knee. In a little the baby finger was placed on the button, and at the signal the current set all the lamps aglow with a beautiful light. The first hush of astonished silence was followed by glad cheers of surprise and wonder from the audience, to most of whom the lightning flash was the only electric light they had ever seen, and had good cause to dread.[19]

The electrical engineer who did most of the work in installing the system was Mr. A.S. Chalmers, who had been a young student at Heriot-Watt in Edinburgh when Laws had been studying there. To him, as a young student,

---

[17] 'Notebook on Electrical Engineering', Laws' Papers, EUL, Special Collections, GEN 563.

[18] Quote by Robert Laws in 'Appeal for the Building Fund of the Livingstonia Mission', pamphlet, October 1903, found in Laws' Papers, EUL Special Collections, GEN 562/6(i).

[19] *United Free Church of Scotland Missionary Record*, March 1906, 117.

Laws seemed like an old man, and Chalmers had been so impressed by him, that he had volunteered to come to Livingstonia.[20]

The Building of the *Gorodi*

And so, back to the Gorodi. As we have already said, none of the other schemes could have been completed without a means of transporting large and heavy equipment from the lakeshore to Khondowe. While Laws had been at home in Scotland in 1900 he had recruited a surveyor for the mission—Mr. F.W. Hardie.[21] With Laws, Hardie began to survey the escarpment from Chitimba to the top of the escarpment, looking for the best route to build a road. Laws had already done this on his own, a couple of years earlier, and Hardie confirmed that most of the route that Laws had chosen was the best way up from the lake.

Hundreds of local people were employed with hoes and shovels to construct the road. I am sure that some of their grandchildren or great-grandchildren are here in the audience today! At particularly difficult or rocky places, where the rocks could not be moved by hand, dynamite had to be used to blast away the obstruction. Work was begun in 1901, but progress was slow. It was not a matter of there being no road today and a road tomorrow. Rather the road was laid out roughly, and then improved as time went on.

On 16th December 1904, Laws wrote to Rev. J. Fairley Daly, Secretary of the Livingstonia committee in Scotland:

> We have had the satisfaction…of having the first wagons with their loads all along the road from the lakeshore to the top of the hill. Oxen could not be trusted in them all the way, and at the narrow parts men had to take them in charge lest any accident might take place. Next dry season, however, three months work will complete the widening of these parts, and make the road complete for through traffic.[22]

The next dry season, by the way, would have been 1905, and if we count it from about May or June, three months work would bring us to August or September; so we can say that the road was completed almost exactly one hundred years ago.

By the time it was completed it stretched in total almost eleven miles and rose two and a half thousand feet six miles between the first hairpin bend and the last. At its broadest it was around twenty feet wide. Originally it had

---

[20] *Laws of Livingstonia*, 299.
[21] Hamish McIntosh, *Robert Laws: Servant of Africa*, 144.
[22] *United Free Church of Scotland Missionary Record*, April 1905, 172.

twenty-two hairpin bends, but over the years this number has been reduced by landslips, so that today there are only twenty bends.

And what about the name of the road? Or, I should say names – for it has two names! The first, official name, which Laws gave to the road, was 'the Longmuir Road'. Longmuir was the name of a lady from Aberdeen who gave Robert Laws £4000 for his work.[23] He decided to use it to build the road, and named the road after the donor. Of course, no one uses that name any more. We all know it as *Gorodi*. So where did that name come from?

Well let me read an extract from Dr. Laws' diary for 1905, which, as I told you earlier, I found just last week.

> On Wednesday 3rd May 1905 I left Livingstonia about 2pm…At the quarry I saw Mr. Sutherland, and then at Manchewe Mr. Gauld, who will likely be away ere I return, and Mr. Adamson. [Further down the] road I met Mr. Hardie, and with him went over the rest of the road, inspecting it carefully with him and arranging for what was needed.[24]

All the names quoted above were those of missionaries working at Livingstonia in 1905. We may have noticed the name of Mr. Hardie, the surveyor, whom I mentioned a little earlier. He did a lot of work on the road, but it is not named after him. A second name Laws mentioned was that of James Gauld. He is not very well known. He worked at Livingstonia as a builder for only five years: between 1900 and 1905.[25] But it is likely that he spent a lot of his time working on the road: perhaps recruiting and overseeing the workers who actually built the road. His name was GAULD; but the local pronunciation was GO-LO-DI. As he was probably the capitao who supervised the actual building of the road, people called it Gauld's road, *Msewu wa Golodi* or just *Golodi*.[26] And the name has remained for one hundred years.

So, as we have seen, what we are remembering here today is not simply a road, but a whole complex of projects which interact with each other. Within a very few years, between 1900-1905, Livingstonia as we see it today took shape. This was the great period of expansion. The Technical School, the Post Office, the Homestead, the Water Supply, the Stone House, the Road, all of these were built. Even the terrace houses where I used to live were built at this time. A few of the prominent buildings we can see today came

---

[23] 'Appeal for the Building Fund of the Livingstonia Mission', Laws' Papers, EUL, Special Collections, GEN 562/6(i); Livingstone, *Laws of Livingstonia*, 304.

[24] Laws' diary, Robert Laws' Papers, EUL, Special Collections.

[25] Donald Fraser, *Livingstonia*, 'List of Missionaries'.

[26] In local pronunciation 'L' and 'R' are virtually interchangeable, so that the name of the road may be spelt either GOLODI or GORODI.

later—the David Gordon Memorial Hospital, the Church, the main educational block (now the Secondary School); but by 1905, one hundred years ago, Livingstonia had basically taken shape; and the key to much of this development was the building of the *Gorodi*.

Historical Critique of Khondowe

But my task, as a historian, is not simply to describe what happened in the past, but to say if and why it was important. Some commentators, both at the time and since have been very full in their praise of what happened here a hundred years ago. Here, for example, is an extract from a pamphlet called *Forty Years in Darkest Africa* written by J.H. Morrison:

> Everything about the place is wonderful. The road that runs up from Florence Bay climbs the seemingly inaccessible height past the waterfall where the Manchewe and the Kazichi drop side by side six hundred feet down the cliff to unite their waters in the gorge below. Graceful avenues of Mlanje cedars crown the summit and link up the various departments of the Institution. The visitor surveys with increasing admiration the variety and efficiency of the workshops where natives are trained to useful industries, the Gordon Memorial Hospital, undoubtedly the finest mission hospital in Africa, the post office with telegraph wires tingling overhead, the turbine house where the waterfall is harnessed and made to supply electric power and light to all the buildings.[27]

But not everyone was so sure. Some of Laws' colleagues at the time felt that the amount of money being used to build the Institution meant that the work at other stations suffered. Donald Fraser asked the question, 'What relation has the whole immense activity and the whole output to tribal life? What relation have all the machinery and the industrial departments to education?'[28] His criticism was even more eloquent in an article he wrote in 1927 when Dr. Laws retired. Speaking of the impression the buildings and roads of Livingstonia made on European visitors, Fraser said, 'Eyes that knew Europe responded to a little bit of Europe, rather than to a sublimated Africa, whose genius they could not understand.'[29]

---

[27] J.H. Morrison, *Forty Years in Darkest Africa: the Story of Dr. Laws of Livingstonia*, Edinburgh, Foreign Mission Committee, United Free Church of Scotland, 1917, 10.

[28] Donald Fraser, 'Remarks on Mr. Ashcroft's Report on his Visit to Livingstonia', Box 1, Livingstonia Papers, National Archives of Malawi, quoted in John McCracken, 'Livingstonia in the Development of Malawi: a Reassessment' in *Bulletin of the Scottish Institute of Missionary Studies,* Vol. 10, 1994, 5.

[29] Donald Fraser, 'Dr. Robert Laws of Livingstonia: a Tribute and an Appreciation' in *The Scots Observer*, 27 August 1927, 9.

W.P. Young, who became Principal of the Overtoun Institution when Laws retired in 1927, also had reservations. Jim Dougall, secretary of the Phelps-Stokes Commission which visited Livingstonia in 1924 recorded that 'He [W.P. Young] feels that the Institution is not serving the native life so much as the European planters.'[30]

More modern historians such as John McCracken, ex-professor of History at Chancellor College, have been critical of the whole enterprise at Livingstonia arguing that it trained a small élite, mainly for colonial or white settler employment, but did very little to raise the general economic standard of the area as a whole.[31]

To some extent I would agree with these criticisms. The whole enterprise was based on the premise (generally accepted by Europeans a century ago) that European culture and technology were clearly superior to African and that Africans must learn the European way if they were to succeed. There was not nearly enough attention given to the question of how the strengths of African society and culture might be used to build a better country and a better Christianity.

In addition, of course, the question of the suitability of the site which Laws chose remains an important issue even today. In 1894 after many missionary deaths at Cape Maclear and Bandawe, the key issue for Laws was finding a healthy site. In retrospect this overrode the question of accessibility. In 1894 the mission actually thought about the possibility of putting the mission headquarters at Ekwendeni, but, at that time, Ekwendeni had only been opened for five years, and Laws felt the Ngoni were still too unsettled to put the mission headquarters among them. And so Mumbwe was chosen. And it remains now, as it did then, a very difficult place to reach and to maintain.

Conclusion

But today we are here to celebrate. To remember what was actually achieved here during this very short period between 1900 and 1905. Central to that achievement was the building of the *Gorodi*. It was the artery through which the life-blood of Livingstonia flowed. And it remains so today, one hundred years after it was built. We call it *Gorodi* after one man who is otherwise forgotten; but in fact, it is a monument to all those many people, most of them unnamed, who helped to build it with their hoes and their shovels, with

---

[30] Journal of J.W.C. Dougall, 26 April 1924, School of Oriental and African Studies, London.

[31] John McCracken, 'Underdevelopment in Malawi: the missionary contribution' in *African Affairs*, 76, 1977.

their toil and their sweat, and to all those who, over the last one hundred years have helped to maintain and repair it.

In spite of its rocks and its gullies; in spite of its bumps and its bends, it always reminds me of the verses from Isaiah 40 (which we also find repeated in Luke 3):

> Nozgani msewu wa Fumu, nyoroskani nthowa zake. Vinkwawu vyose viwundike, mapiri ghose na tumapiri vidilimukire pasi. Vyakubendera vyose viti vizgokenge vyakunyoroka, nthowa za mabonkhobonkho zizamuskesketeka. Ndipo wantu wose wizamuwona chiponosko cha Chiuta.[32]

> Get the road ready for the Lord; make a straight path for him to travel! Every valley must be filled up, every hill and mountain levelled off. The winding roads must be made straight and the rough paths made smooth, [so that] all mankind will see God's salvation.[33]

For me, this sums up what Robert Laws, and all those who helped him build the *Gorodi* were trying to do. They were preparing the way for the Lord. Our presence here today in such numbers[34] shows that their work was not in vain.

---

[32] *Phangano Liphya,* Luka 3: 4-6, pages 165-66; Blantyre, Bible Society of Malawi, 2002.

[33] Luke 3: 4-6, (Good News Bible).

[34] Approximately five hundred people attended the centenary lecture. Several times that number, perhaps two thousand, attended the celebrations as a whole.

'Bloodthirsty Savages' or 'Stout-hearted Zulus'?: Ambivalent Missionary Attitudes to Ngoni Violence in the Late Nineteenth Century.[1]

Introduction

In the context of the early years of the Livingstonia mission in Malawi in the last quarter of the nineteenth century, the question of missionary attitudes to various kinds of African violence in the area in which they were working, is a particularly fascinating one. In this paper, I want to concentrate specifically on missionary attitudes towards war, raiding and violence on the part of the Ngoni people of northern Malawi, who, by the First World War, made up the largest—and one might reasonably claim, the strongest—part of the burgeoning Presbyterian church in northern Malawi; but who, a mere generation previously, had generally been regarded as a warlike people particularly resistant to the call of the Christian gospel.

What I want to do in this paper, is to explore the ambivalent missionary attitudes to Ngoni violence, and to try to indicate the basis on which these attitudes emerged. Since it is my purpose here to look specifically at *missionary* attitudes to violence, I will deliberately exclude (except occasionally, in passing) African sources commenting on Ngoni violence. Needless to say, any more general or more lengthy study of the topic would, necessarily need to concentrate heavily on African sources, including the views of the Ngoni themselves.

M'mbelwa's Ngoni (sometimes known as the northern Ngoni) had arrived in what is now the Mzimba district of Malawi in around 1855, having migrated from the area of Lake St. Lucia in KwaZulu, beginning around 1820.[2] Most nineteenth century European commentators identified them as Zulu, though this is really an anachronism, since, at the time of the beginning of their migration, the Zulu were merely one of many clans of the Nguni peoples of south-eastern Africa. It would be more accurate to describe

[1] This paper was first delivered as the Keynote Address at a conference on 'War and Peace in the History of Missions', held in Edinburgh in July 1998 under the auspices of the Yale-Edinburgh Consultation on the History of Missions, and is published here for the first time.
[2] See Thompson, *Christianity in Northern Malawi*, chapter 1, 'Ngoni Origins'. For an Ngoni account of their origins, see Yesaya Chibambo, 'Makani gha waNgoni' in *Midauko*, Livingstonia, 1965.

the Ngoni as belonging to the Ndwandwe branch of the Nguni peoples, and as speaking a language somewhere between Zulu and Xhosa, though nearer to the former. Some elements of the group which soon coalesced around Zwangendaba may also be described as Swazi.

In a comparatively short paper such as this, there is no space to look in any detail at the origins of their migration—not least because some strands of recent South African historiography query the whole idea of the *Mfecane*[3] as being a major cause of mass migrations such as that of the Ngoni. Suffice it to say here that a group comprising not more than a few hundred Ngoni, led by Zwangendaba Jere, left KwaZulu around 1820, and began a slow, gradual movement northwards, during which they assimilated many people along the way, and eventually moved as far north as southern Tanzania—where Zwangendaba died around 1847. The group then splintered, and the major section, now led by M'mbelwa Jere, moved south into Malawi, where they settled around 1855.

The Ngoni were predominantly pastoralists, and during the long migration had become accustomed to a pattern of life centred around raiding other tribes—both to obtain food, and to capture and incorporate extra personnel into their social structure.

First Missionary Contacts

The first missionary to make reference to the Ngoni was David Livingstone, who came across the effects of their raiding during his exploration in 1859 up the west side of Lake Malawi[4] (which he had first called Nyenyezi, meaning 'stars', and then Nyassa). Livingstone referred to the Ngoni by the names given to them by other local tribes—a good indication that much of his information was second hand, and called them variously the *Maviti* and the *Mazitu*.[5] Though Livingstone's comments are comparatively brief, three features which were to be common in much missionary description of the Ngoni over the next thirty years, are already discernible. The first is the impression of the extreme destructiveness of Ngoni raids. Livingstone spoke of seeing near Mankhambira's village, close to what was later to become the Scottish mission station of Bandawe, 'the putrid bodies of many who had

[3] For a discussion of the *Mfecane* ('Time of Troubles') see Carolyn Hamilton (ed.), *The Mfecane Aftermath*, Johannesburg, Witwatersrand University Press, 1995.
[4] David and Charles Livingstone, *Narrative of an Expedition to the Zambezi and its Tributaries*, London, 1865.
[5] *Ibid.*, 381.

fallen by Mazitu spears only a few days before'.[6] But secondly, he commented that some sort of alliance with the Ngoni might be mutually beneficial: 'They would be most efficient allies to the English, and might themselves be benefited by more intercourse.'[7] The third was a comment on the Ngoni and the slave trade—a somewhat controversial topic in later years. Livingstone's reports that the Ngoni never sold those captured in raids, but incorporated them into their own social structures.[8] Though Livingstone claims to have met some Ngoni, he also admits that they were local people who had been incorporated into Ngoni society.

It was to be another sixteen years before the Scottish missionaries of the Livingstonia mission arrived in Malawi, yet what is interesting is how closely their comments on the Ngoni mirror those of Livingstone. E.D. Young, the leader of the first party to reach Lake Malawi with the steamer *Ilala* in 1875, writing a couple of years later, described the Ngoni as 'this desperate horde, whose terror is known throughout a vast portion of Africa'.[9] Yet, like Livingstone, he went on to comment on the advantages of an alliance, 'If we once get on friendly terms with the Maviti there is no end to the influence it may have on future events for Central Africa'.[10] Livingstone's third point— the involvement, or non-involvement of the Ngoni in the slave trade—was also a matter of comment among early Scottish missionaries, with the balance of opinion firmly on the side of non-involvement. George Williams, the last of the Xhosa evangelists from Lovedale (who worked among the Ngoni between 1884 and 1888) made an interesting distinction, commenting that there had been a limited amount of secretive slave-trading, and adding, 'I say underhand buying of slaves, because none of the real Ngoni does it. It is carried on by their freed slaves.'[11] This, in its turn, leads to another fascinating distinction made by the missionaries, between slave trading, and the capture during Ngoni raiding of captives who became *abafo*—a term sometimes translated as 'domestic slaves', but which might more accurately be translated as 'retainers' or 'serfs'. Surprisingly, the very missionaries who were, on the whole strongly opposed to Ngoni raiding in general (as we shall see below) regarded the institution of *abafo* with comparative toleration. Angus Elmslie (who was to become most famous to

---

[6] *Ibid.*
[7] *Ibid.*, 128.
[8] *Ibid.*, 385.
[9] E.D. Young, *Nyassa: a Journal of Adventures*, London, 1877, 177.
[10] *Ibid.*, 212.
[11] George Williams to Laws, December 1884, Shepperson collection.

the Scottish public in general for his book *Among the Wild Ngoni*, first published in 1899) wrote in 1891 'The position of the [domestic] slaves is not devoid of comfort. ... They are well-treated, and, as no slaves are sold, they enjoy the fruit of their own labours and live in peace.'[12] Donald Fraser (himself the author of a book on the Ngoni entitled *Winning a Primitive People*) wrote at the turn of the century that 'their position is not a hard one. If they are discontented they can change masters. They give their masters a little free labour, and in return are made members of his family.'[13]

First Livingstonia Contacts with M'mbelwa

In approaching the question of Scottish missionary attitudes to the northern Ngoni, and particularly in relation to violence and war, one cannot escape comment on the very first missionary contact with paramount chief M'mbelwa in December 1878. It occurred shortly after the missionaries had opened a settlement at Kaning'ina on the edge of Ngoni territory. M'mbelwa summoned the missionaries to his village to hear why the mission had come. Two missionaries went to meet him: the Scottish agriculturalist Alexander Riddel, and the Xhosa evangelist William Koyi. On 20th December 1878, Riddel, ill with fever, struggled out of his tent to meet M'mbelwa. We are fortunate to have his account of what he said:

> At noon I got up and called them to the tent door and told them whence we had come—from a far off country full of every good thing—for what we had come—to give the people of this country God's message to them. I showed them a Bible and told them it was it that made our nation rich and powerful, and that now one of their own tribe [William Koyi] had come to tell them what the Book had done for him and his people in their own old country. I then gave a sample of the commandments and some of the leading virtues it inculcated. I said that if they received it, it would make them wise and happy and teach them how to become wealthy by fair means not by robbery etc.[14]

Two things are significant about this presentation. The first is that Riddel (and the missionaries in general) regarded the Ngoni policy of raiding as a form of robbery. The second is that the gospel was presented to the Ngoni leadership as an alternative way of becoming rich and powerful. A few months earlier, during what was the first substantive contact between the northern Ngoni and the mission (when a group of missionaries met the

---

[12] Elmslie, *Introductory Grammar of the Ngoni (Zulu) Language*, Aberdeen, 1891, 'Introduction', x.

[13] Fraser, 'The Zulu of Nyasaland' in *Proceedings of the Philosophical Society of Glasgow*, Vol.XXXII, 1900-01, 66.

[14] Kaning'ina Journal, 20 December 1878, Ms. 7910, National Library of Scotland.

headman Chiputula Nhlane at his village of Njuyu) one of the group—the civil engineer James Stewart—wrote the following in his journal:

> We astonished them by our rifles and revolvers. I twice emptied my revolver at a tree into a space that I could cover with my hand. Distance about fifteen yards. They did not very much like it and said that I was now chief.[15]

Though the missionaries may have felt able to make a clear distinction between the type of 'innocent' violence with which Stewart impressed the Ngoni, and the 'immoral' violence in which the Ngoni themselves were involved, such moral distinctions may not have been so obvious to the Ngoni themselves.

Missionary Attitudes to Ngoni Raiding

For the first eight or nine years of contact between the Scottish missionaries and the northern Ngoni comments on Ngoni raiding were almost entirely negative—often couched in quite extreme language. The following example (though taken from a slightly later period) would not be untypical of the kind of comment which was regularly made at this time. The Scottish cleric J. W. Jack (though he had never been to Africa) described Ngoni raiding as 'the bloodthirsty cruelty that was constantly taking place in this land of darkness and savagery'.[16] Such views, of course, he had gathered from missionary correspondence and publications, and they were to be repeated retrospectively by several of the Scottish missionaries in their writings. and the official Livingstonia Mission handbook, published in 1903, spoke of the Ngoni as 'bloodthirsty savages.utterly regardless of life.'[17] The first British Commissioner of Malawi, H.H. Johnston, writing in 1890, went even further, describing the Ngoni in print as 'blood-thirsty wild beasts'.[18]

There can be no doubt that the raiding which formed an important part of Ngoni social, economic and political life in the late nineteenth century was a violent and often brutal activity (as all war is) and that many innocent people suffered as a result of it. Yet neither the violence itself, nor, indeed, the missionary reaction to it, are as straightforward as might at first appear. In the Scottish mission literature of the early 1880s (and even in much later accounts of the same period) there emerged what might almost be described

---

[15] Jack Thompson (editor), *From Nyassa to Tanganyika: the Journal of James Stewart CE in Central Africa 1876-1879*, Blantyre, 1989, 62.

[16] J.W. Jack, *Daybreak in Livingstonia*, Edinburgh, Oliphant, Anderson and Ferrier, 1901, 99.

[17] *Livingstonia Handbook*, Edinburgh, United Free Church of Scotland, 1903.

[18] H.H. Johnston, 'The Development of Tropical Africa under British Auspices' in *The Fortnightly Review*, 1 November 1890, 704.

as a template of violence in northern Malawi. This early missionary over-simplification may be summarised as follows: on the lakeshore lived a peaceful and industrious people—the Tonga, whom David Livingstone had first encountered in 1859. When the missionaries settled amongst them, first with an experimental station in 1878, and then by moving the mission head-quarters to Bandawe in 1881, the Tonga welcomed them, and were keen to learn of Christianity. In the hills lived the 'war-like' Ngoni, who were resis-tant to the demands of the gospel, and who preyed on and raided the sur-rounding tribes without provocation, for crops, cattle and people.

While it needs to be admitted immediately that raiding was indeed a major element in Ngoni society at this period, and that suffering and death were often involved, several factors need to be taken into consideration. To begin with, the purpose of Ngoni raiding was primarily economic, rather than military. It was aimed at strengthening the Ngoni state through the incorporation of new captives, and the seizure of cattle and food. Accounts which speak of the wholesale slaughter of men and women simply do not make sense. In the long term, the success of Ngoni raiding depended upon leaving behind enough adult food producers to ensure the continuation of crops and cattle as the targets of future raids. Where killing became indis-criminate (and there is evidence that it occasionally did) it was the result of the break-down of the Ngoni policy of raiding, rather than of the policy itself, and was often carried out by incorporated serfs of the Ngoni (many of Tonga origin themselves) as opposed to the Zansi-Ngoni[19] who formed the political élite.

It is also important to realise that almost all missionary accounts of Ngoni raiding at this period came to them through the Tonga themselves, and that the Tonga had a vested interest in exaggerating the extent of Ngoni violence, and the innocence of their own reactions. What was going on in the early 1880s, was a struggle between the Tonga and the Ngoni for the economic, religious, magical and (it was hoped) diplomatic support of the Scottish mis-sionaries. On the one hand, once the missionaries had established their head-quarters at Bandawe on the lakeshore in 1881, the Tonga wanted to use their presence to strengthen their own position. On the other hand the Ngoni (among whom the missionaries settled permanently in 1882) would have preferred a missionary withdrawal from the lakeshore, to give them a freer hand to attack the Tonga, and more complete access to missionary alliance.

---

[19] Here and elsewhere, I have used the term 'Zansi-Ngoni' to refer to those Ngoni—the *abaZansi*—who were part of the original group coming from the south-east, or joined soon after the migration began.

Two things emerge from a detailed study of the missionary archives of the period. The first is that Tonga reports of anticipated Ngoni raids did not always materialise. A day to day reading of the Bandawe mission journal indicates that many Tonga reports were false alarms. Secondly, it is clear that raiding was a two-way process, in which the Tonga were far from being merely the innocent victims. Robert Laws, writing many years later in his *Reminiscences of Livingstonia* recalls that during one early missionary expedition

> we came to what was an old village occupied previously by one of their [Ngoni] Chiefs and his people, but being near the Lumpasa Valley it was liable to sudden attacks from the Tonga, who destroyed their gardens and property. This led the Angoni to go further westwards.[20]

But such accounts were not simply afterthoughts, given after the advantage of several decades of reflection. Occasionally they also appear contemporaneously. In 1882, for example, Laws writes of groups of Tonga attacking outlying hill villages in order to capture slaves.[21] In spite of all the above, the overall picture painted by the missionaries in the early 1880s was predominantly one-sided, and anti-Ngoni.

At first sight the simple explanation of this might seem to be that the missionaries were in favour of peace, and opposed to war and violence. This, however, is much too simplistic. As the 1880s wore on, Ngoni opportunities to raid the lakeshore were restricted by the missionary presence at Bandawe, by an earlier promise of M'mbelwa not to attack Bandawe while the missionaries were there, and by the increasing ability of the Tonga to defend themselves through the building of stockaded villages, and the acquisition of guns. The Ngoni began to turn their attention in other directions—to the north-west, and to the south. 1887 was a crucial year in Ngoni-mission relations, and in missionary attitudes to Ngoni violence. One would only briefly add here, by way of background, that for several months during 1887 the missionaries both at Njuyu among the Ngoni, and at Bandawe on the lakeshore, were in fear for their lives, and that at both places missionaries evacuated essential supplies, anticipating the possibility of having to withdraw altogether.[22] At one point, the Tonga even held the missionaries as hostages for several weeks, refusing to allow them to leave Bandawe—fearful that they would abandon them in favour of the Ngoni.[23]

[20] Robert Laws, *Reminiscences of Livingstonia*, Edinburgh, 1934, 72.
[21] Letter from Dr. Laws, *Free Church of Scotland Monthly*, September 1882, 270.
[22] Thompson, *Christianity*, 53-59.
[23] Bandawe Journal, 17 September to 17 October 1887, Ms. 7911, NLS.

At the same time, however, the Ngoni were contemplating military expeditions in other areas, and it is the missionary reaction to this which concerns us here. Early on in 1887, it is clear that the Ngoni were beginning to worry about possible military alliances against them from other sources. In particular, they seem to have been concerned about an alliance between the Bemba of north-eastern Zambia, and the Swahili-Arabs who were involved in slave-trading at the north end of lake Malawi. In September, possibly in order to forestall a joint attack, the Ngoni sent out a large army, which, in alliance with Senga and Bisa forces from eastern Zambia, defeated the Bemba at Kabondwe, and killed the Bemba chief Ndakala.[24]

The missionary reaction to this attack is interesting. Whereas previously the whole concept of Ngoni raiding had been condemned, now Elmslie wrote that

> the Ngoni are the only people who are able to meet Arab invasion, and it may be that they will be used of God to stem the tide of Islamism which threatens to swamp all lawful trading and our beloved Livingstonia Mission.[25]

Such a change of attitude was also reflected in the pages of *The Free Church Monthly*, the official organ of the Free Church of Scotland. In June 1887 it had been talking of 'taming the wild Ngoni'; a year later it was referring to them as 'that stout-hearted tribe of Zulus'.[26] At the time, a motley bunch of Europeans were planning a military campaign against the slave trader Mlozi at the north end of the lake—a campaign eventually led by the young Frederick Lugard, who was seriously wounded in the encounter. Following the Ngoni success against the Bemba, the possibility of the Europeans asking the Ngoni to help them against the Swahili-Arabs was seriously contemplated, and actually supported by Elmslie. In the end the Ngoni were not recruited, though a small band of Ngoni warriors did clash separately with Mlozi's followers in October 1888.[27]

In these events (and not least in Elmslie's quote above) can be seen a considerable shift in missionary attitudes to Ngoni violence. When the mission itself was not threatened, and when the object of Ngoni attack was a group or a cause to which the missionaries were opposed, then the violence

---

[24] Elmslie to Laws, 12 & 24 September 1887, Ms. 7890, NLS, and Andrew Roberts, *A History of the Bemba*, London, 1973, 376.

[25] Elmslie, 27 December 1887, quoted in an unidentified article entitled 'The Arab Attack on Free Church Missionaries' found at Ms. 7906, NLS.

[26] *Free Church of Scotland Monthly*, June 1887, 179; and August 1888, 139. One has to bear in mind at this period, a lapse of several months, between events on the ground in Malawi, and their publication in Scotland.

[27] Elmslie to Laws, 22 October 1888, Ms. 7891, NLS.

was not only acceptable, but actually attributable to the will of God. The Bemba were seen to be involved in the slave trade, and to be in league with the Swahili-Arabs at the north end of the lake. Thus, two of the favourite targets of missionary opposition—the slave trade and the spread of Islam were seen to be thwarted by the Ngoni victory at Kabondwe; the fact that Ngoni motivation for the attack was quite different from European seems not even to have been considered. Put bluntly, Ngoni violence could be justified insofar as it seemed to be in line with the political, economic and cultural priorities of the missionaries, and was not targeted against Europeans or their allies. A few years later a strange series of events took place in *uNgoni*, involving Ngoni, missionaries, European traders and colonial government, in which these parameters were tested to the full.

The Ziehl Case

In January 1899 an employee of the North Charterland Exploration Company, William Robert Ziehl, entered *uNgoni* with a group of African employees in order to buy cattle. When he left hurriedly a few weeks later the area was in uproar, with the Ngoni accusing Ziehl and his followers of murder, rape, theft and various other offences. These events, and the trial which followed four months later, had a profound effect on Ngoni, mission and government in their relationships with one another, and did much to prepare the way for the eventual annexation of *uNgoni* by the British in 1904.

The affair had its origins in the rinderpest epidemic of 1893, which swept through Malawi from the north and on down into Zimbabwe. Although Ngoni herds were badly affected they seem to have made a quick recovery, and by 1894 Europeans were already coming into the district from outside to buy cattle.[28] Early in 1895 Elmslie warned Laws that

> now is our time to lay in stock because the people are poor and from Blantyre we may expect white men up for cattle this dry season, and if so prices will be at least trebled, judging from what some have already paid last season.[29]

At the beginning of 1895 a bull could be bought in *uNgoni* for around one pound (or its equivalent in cloth); by the end of the year some Europeans were paying 2.10s.0d. [£2-50] and by January 1896 as much as £4.[30]

By the end of 1896 prices seemed to have dropped off a little, but the next couple of years saw the beginning of an influx of Europeans into Malawi—many of them from Mashonaland. The growing trouble which this

---

[28] Elmslie to Laws, 21 January 1895, Elmslie File, NLS.

[29] *Ibid.*

[30] *Ibid.*, 27 November 1895 & 14 January 1896.

immigration caused was indicated by the fact that, by the end of 1898, the colonial administration was, for the first time, forced to employ a European warder at Blantyre prison—a development which Sharpe linked directly with the influx of Europeans from Mashonaland.[31] *The Central African Times* of 26 November 1898 reported that European cattle buyers from outside the country had caused trouble in Chiwere's district by taking 120 head of cattle for which they paid only £25 in goods.[32] The widespread nature of the problem and its effect on Africans in general can be seen by the fact that the porters of a European visitor to Mpezeni's early in 1899 were told by local police near Mlangeni 'Oh we know where your *Msungu* is going, he is a dog going to steal cattle'.[33] The northern Ngoni were not immune from this trouble either, and on several occasions the missionaries had been called in to deal with minor disputes involving cattle buyers or gold prospectors in the area.[34]

The impact of Ziehl, who arrived in *uNgoni* in January 1899, was far from minor. He was originally from Natal, and was employed by the North Charterland Exploration Company, with its headquarters near the village of the Ngoni chief Mpezeni, whose village of Mlangeni was near the present day town of Chipata in eastern Zambia. This in itself was enough to arouse suspicion against Ziehl and his band of local followers, some of whom were armed, for following the military defeat of Mpezeni in January 1898 by a British force under the command of Captain Brake, and which included artillery and Maxim guns, the northern Ngoni were intensely suspicious of any European who had been in Mpezeni's area at the time of the war.[35]

Ziehl's account of the events which followed his arrival in *uNgoni* may be summarised as follows. He arrived in the country in January 1899, with a group of African employees and five guns, two of which belonged to the North Charterland Company police. His followers later brought him ten guns they had found hidden in a hole and he confiscated others from Africans with no permits. He was at first well received, bought a number of cattle, and exchanged presents with numerous chiefs. When he came to Julizga's village he sent some of his followers to the village for grass. They were beaten, and

---

[31] Sharpe to Foreign Office, 14 February 1899, FO2/208, National Archives of United Kingdom (NAUK), London.

[32] *Central African Times*, 26 November 1898, 1.

[33] *Ibid.,* 8 April 1899, 5.

[34] *Ibid.,* 8 April 1899, 5; and Fraser, *Primitive People*, 102.

[35] *Central African Times*, 25 April 1899, 5.

Julizga later apologised and said his villagers were drunk; he sold two cattle to Ziehl.

On 18 January some mission teachers led by Daniel Nhlane arrived at Julizga's. They had no guns or spears, but were carrying knobkerries and umbrellas. According to Ziehl Daniel Nhlane asked him why he was buying cattle in mission territory and told him to go away. Ziehl said he had a licence to buy cattle. Nhlane replied 'This is Mission country. It does not belong to the Administration. You must go.' Ziehl told him to go back to his employer and report what he had said. Nhlane replied that he

> was not going to be told to go by any white man in his own country. Ziehl claims that he was then struck several times by Nhlane and some others, as a result of which he sustained a fractured skull and fell down semi-conscious. He fired five shots but hit no one. After that he left the country.[36]

The Ngoni account of what happened differed substantially from Ziehl's in several important respects. First of all the trouble did not start at Julizga's but much earlier. The Ngoni accused Ziehl and his followers of forcing the sale of cattle against the will of their owners, seizing cattle without payment, whipping villagers with a *chikoti*, and raping several women.[37]

A second major difference of emphasis was in what took place during Nhlane's interview with Ziehl. According to the Ngoni account eleven mission employees went to see Ziehl. They treated him with courtesy and respect, but he lost his temper and began to beat Daniel Nhlane with his *chikoti*. Nhlane hit him on the arm and then ran away; another member of the party—identified only as David (possibly Zinyoka) then hit him hard on the head and one or two others hit him. Ziehl pulled out his revolver and fired repeatedly at them. Two of the Ngoni were slightly wounded.[38] In further disturbances on his way out of the area, Ziehl's followers shot and killed two men and wounded an old woman, though Ziehl claimed 'he told them not to fire on the natives'.[39]

The particular interest and importance of the Ziehl case lies not only in the way the Ngoni reacted to the extreme provocations of Ziehl's stay in *uNgoni*, but to the way in which both the mission and the administration became involved in the case and in the Ngoni reaction to that involvement.

---

[36] The above account is based on Ziehl's evidence at his trial, as found in Sharpe to Foreign Office (No. 145) Minutes of Ziehl case, 26 June 1899, FO 2/209, NAUK; and *Central African Times*, 24 June 1899, 6-7, 'The Zichl Case' *(Sic)*. Throughout the case the *Central African Times* spells the name incorrectly as ZICHL.

[37] *Central African Times*, 25 April 1899, 5.

[38] Minutes of the Ziehl Case, FO 2/209, NAUK.

[39] *Central African Times*, 24 June 1899, 7.

Mission involvement was centred almost entirely on the person of Donald Fraser, who at the time was the only European missionary in *uNgoni*. Fraser was at Ekwendeni at the time, and the main events of the drama took place near Engalaweni, around twenty miles away, so that his first contacts with the affair were by messenger and letter.[40]

Having heard several reports of violence, rape and theft Fraser sent a letter to Daniel Nhlane, asking him to find out if they were true. This led to Nhlane's confrontation with Ziehl on 18th January. As soon as Fraser heard about this on the following day, he sent a message to C.A. Cardew, the Collector at the lakeshore, asking him to arrest the white man,[41] and to paramount chief Mbalekelwa and the local teachers, urging them to do nothing until Cardew arrived. On Friday and Saturday further messages arrived, telling of the recovery of fifty or sixty cattle by a party which had set out in pursuit, and the killing of two men by Ziehl's followers when they returned to try to recover the cattle left behind.

Up to this point Fraser seems to have been uncertain about his own involvement in the affair. He claims that this was because he was the lone European at Ekwendeni, and didn't want to leave the station,[42] but it was probably because, at the time, he was a young missionary who had been in Malawi for just two years, and also, perhaps, because he was reluctant to break too sharply with the mission tradition of non-interference in civil affairs.

The arrival of messengers from chiefs Mbalekelwa and Mzukuzuku on Saturday 21 January, saying that unless he came immediately they could no longer restrain their armies from going in pursuit of Ziehl, finally convinced Fraser of the full seriousness of the situation. The arrival of another Scottish missionary, William Murray, from the mission station at Khondowe freed Fraser to leave Ekwendeni, but it wasn't until 3 p.m. the following Tuesday that he finally arrived at Engalaweni, (accompanied by Dr. Scott who had come up from Bandawe on hearing of the trouble).

---

[40] Fraser wrote four main accounts of the Ziehl case: *Central African Times*, 15 April 1899, 5-6; *United Free Church of Scotland Missionary Record*, [*UFCSMR*], April 1901, 156-8; *Winning a Primitive People*, 101-09; and *Autobiography of an African,* 146-53. The fullest of these accounts is his letter in the *Central African Times*, and the account which follows is based on that, unless otherwise footnoted.

[41] Note that, from a colonial point of view *uNgoni* presented something of an anomaly. Although in general terms, the British colonial authorities claimed jurisdiction over the whole of what is now Malawi, they had not yet occupied *uNgoni* and did not do so until 1904. The Ngoni still considered themselves to be an independent nation.

[42] *UFCSMR*, April 1901, 157.

At Engalaweni Fraser heard many of the complaints against Ziehl in detail for the first time, and also the Ngoni complaint that 'we [i.e. the mission] would not allow them to punish evil-doers'. The fact that they made this complaint shows just how high Ngoni feelings on the matter were running; the fact that they did not send out an army in spite of these feelings, indicates both their considerable restraint, and the extensive influence of the mission in *uNgoni*.

Fraser reacted to what he was told by suggesting that an *impi* of specially chosen warriors should be sent out in pursuit of Ziehl. He suggested that he and Scott should accompany the army, and laid down four conditions which the Ngoni accepted. These were:

> that we ourselves should pick the men, that no beer should be touched on the road, that we should be absolutely obeyed, and that no one but ourselves should have any contact with the white man.

As final preparations for the pursuit were being made on Tuesday night, news arrived that Cardew was finally on his way from the lakeshore. He arrived the following evening, and thus averted by a few hours what would have been the unprecedented sight of a Scottish missionary leading out an Ngoni army.

Though Cardew and his police, accompanied by a special detachment of chief Mzukuzuku's men gave chase, Ziehl was already out of the country, having returned to Mpezeni's area. In assessing Fraser's part in the affair up to this juncture several points could be made. First, he found himself the victim of a conflict of loyalties. His allegiance to the British judicial system made him very reluctant to let the Ngoni take the law into their own hands; Fraser was concerned that Ziehl might be a British subject, and that any unilateral action against him by the Ngoni, might bring down the colonial weight of the British administration on the Ngoni people as a whole. At the same time it did not prevent him from becoming directly involved in the affair, to an extent with which Elmslie, on leave at the time, was not entirely happy.[43] Again, Fraser's concern to protect the Ngoni from possible criticism led him, in his two accounts of the affair which were published more or less contemporaneously with the event, to play down considerably the amount of violence which the Ngoni had inflicted on Ziehl.[44] His later accounts, by contrast, particularly the chapter 'A Filibuster' in *Autobiogra-*

---

[43] Elmslie to Laws, 20 May 1899, Elmslie File, NLS.
[44] *Central African Times*, 15 April 1899, 5-6; and *UFCSMR*, April 1901, 156-58.

phy of an African[45] relate the events in some detail even, one suspects, with a trace of relish.

The escape of Ziehl to Mpezeni's was by no means the end of the affair; indeed, in terms of the involvement of the administration it was only the beginning. Cardew's report on the events, prepared and sent off to Commissioner Sharpe (the chief colonial official in Nyasaland) within a week of the escape of Ziehl, recommended the placing of a government official in *uNgoni* to prevent similar trouble in the future.[46] Two more immediate results, however, were the introduction by Sharpe in February 1899 of the 'Purchase of Cattle from Natives Ordinance' and his taking up of Ziehl's case with Codrington, deputy administrator of north-eastern Rhodesia.

The Purchase of Cattle from Natives Ordinance' which was gazetted as an urgent measure on 24th February 1899,[47] is almost certainly directly connected with Ziehl's behaviour in *uNgoni*. Though too late to be of any immediate value to the Ngoni, it sought to protect Africans from unscrupulous dealers such as Ziehl, by laying down that in certain districts, including West Nyasa (of which *uNgoni*, from a British perspective, was then technically a part) no cattle could be purchased without a permit issued by the Collector. In applying for a permit a prospective cattle buyer had to state the number of cattle he intended to buy, the minimum price he expected to pay for them, and the chiefs from whose areas he hoped to purchase them. Before leaving the district he had to appear before the Collector to satisfy him that the purchases had been above board. Though possibly under preparation for some time, the introduction of these regulations on an urgent basis less than a month after Sharpe received Cardew's report, at least indicates the seriousness with which the Administration viewed the Ziehl case.

So too does the fact that Sharpe took up the matter with Codrington, Administrator of north-eastern Rhodesia, during a subsequent visit to Fort Jameson [modern Chipata] in the course of which he presented Codrington with a warrant for Ziehl's arrest to answer charges in connection with his behaviour in *uNgoni* in January.[48] As a result of Sharpe's discussions with Codrington, however, Ziehl had first of all to appear at Fort Jameson, charged with illegally raising a police force. The manager of the North Charterland Company had been on leave in Europe since October 1898, and

[45] Fraser, *Autobiography*, 146-54.
[46] Report from C.A. Cardew to Sharpe, January 1899, FO 2/208, NAUK.
[47] *Ibid., British Central Africa Gazette*, 24 February 1899, Colonial Office 541/1, NAUK.
[48] Sharpe to FO, 8 May 1899, FO 2/208, NAUK.

Sharpe commented that the acting manager Hayes 'appears to be a weak man in poor health and to have allowed Ziehl to obtain entire control of the local affairs of the North Charterland Company'.[49] As a result Ziehl had raised, uniformed and armed a force of company police when in fact he had no legal right to do so. The outcome was that the entire African police force was imprisoned for a short time at Fort Jameson, while Ziehl was merely fined £5 by Codrington[50]—in itself a comment on the grossly unbalanced racial attitudes in the administration of colonial justice in the area at the time.

One other action of Sharpe at this time is perhaps worth noting—if only in contrast to Codrington's action above. Having appointed Captain F.B. Pearce, the assistant deputy commissioner for British Central Africa (Nyasaland), to hear the case against Ziehl at Ekwendeni, Sharpe instructed him that 'should the evidence justify a conviction, a heavy fine or a term of imprisonment should be inflicted'. 'It is absolutely necessary' he added in his report to the Foreign Office, 'to put a stop to lawless proceedings on the part of Europeans in these districts lying west of Lake Nyasa.'[51]

Sharpe himself had earlier noted the connection between a large influx of Europeans, and the outbreak of trouble at Mpezeni's. He seemed determined to prevent the same thing happening again—this time in the territory for which he was responsible.

The Trial of Ziehl

The trial of Ziehl took place at Ekwendeni between 25 and 27 May 1899. Pearce sat as judge, together with two assessors—Andrew Forbes, a trader from Bandawe, and William Murray the Livingstonia missionary.[52] Ziehl was charged with nine offences, including several involving assault on various Ngoni (one of whom was Daniel Nhlane) and one involving the theft of cattle and goats. The most serious charges were that he levied war against the Ngoni, and that he illegally armed the Africans travelling with him. It is interesting to note that in the very full account it gave of the trial, the *Central African Times* made no mention of these latter two charges.[53]

---

[49] *Ibid.*

[50] *Ibid.*

[51] *Ibid.*

[52] The main account of Ziehl's trial is in Sharpe to FO (no. 145), minutes of the Ziehl case, 16 June 1899, FO 2/209, NAUK. Only references to sources other than this will be footnoted in my account of the trial.

[53] *Central African Times*, 24 June 1899, 6-7.

Much of the evidence at the trial hinged on the nature of the meeting of 18 January between Ziehl and Daniel Nhlane. Ziehl tried to argue that he had told Nhlane clearly that he had a licence to trade, and that Nhlane had told him in return that he had no right to trade in mission territory—even with a government permit. All the Ngoni witnesses denied both these allegations, and indeed, one outstanding feature of the trial was the consistency of the Ngoni evidence. In spite of detailed cross-examination by Ziehl, they all stuck doggedly to their account, which agreed on almost every point.

Another facet of the trial turned on the African's approach to the European, and concerned the question of whether or not Daniel Nhlane and his group had taken off their hats when they approached the white man. Ziehl, drawing on the inherent racism of much of the social custom of the time, pinned his hopes of acquittal on such trifles, but once again, the Ngoni witnesses were insistent that they had approached Ziehl in a respectful and deferential manner.

Among those giving evidence were Chimtunga [Mbalekelwa] paramount chief of the northern Ngoni, and the veteran missionary Elmslie, who, although not in *uNgoni* during the disturbances, was asked to comment on the general state of the country. Their evidence was remarkably similar. Chimtunga remarked that 'The Angoni had never previously attacked a white man, and would not wish to attack a white man if he had not done much wrong to the people.'

Elmslie had earlier given it as his opinion that 'He believed they would have to receive very great provocation before attacking a white man.' Both the Ngoni and the missionaries carefully avoided mention of the fact that Daniel Nhlane had, on one occasion several years earlier, attacked the missionary Charles Stuart with a shield and spear, after he had been dismissed as a mission foreman.[54]

In his summing-up Pearce made two criticisms of what may be termed the Ngoni side. First of all he criticised Fraser for sending Daniel Nhlane to Ziehl[55] on the grounds that 'it was injudicious to send a native to enquire into a white man's doings'. Secondly he claimed that though Ziehl had been wrong to assault Nhlane 'yet he had some degree of provocation'. Both these

---

[54] Fraser, *Autobiography*, 73.

[55] Fraser's evidence on this point is somewhat contradictory. In the *Missionary Record*, April 1901, 156, he claims that he did not send Daniel Nhlane to Ziehl, but only to find out from the local Ngoni if the rumours of outrages were true. This version seems to agree with his accounts in *Central African Times, Autobiography of an African,* and *Winning a Primitive People.* Giving evidence at the trial, however, he stated that he had given Daniel a letter for Ziehl, which Daniel had failed to deliver.

opinions were soon to be subjected to criticism. Nevertheless, he came down overwhelmingly against Ziehl, finding him guilty on eight of the nine charges, and sentencing him to six months imprisonment or a fine of £50. He was also ordered to pay a total of £9.10s.0d. to those he had wronged. (This included compensation of £1.10s.0d. for the families of each of the two men killed by his followers.)

Ziehl paid his fine and compensation, had those cattle returned to him which no one else had claimed, and left the area the next day.[56] He was eventually expelled from the country for a repetition of the offence.[57] Difficult though it is to make comparisons, there is little doubt that Ziehl escaped very lightly. He had certainly cause to be grateful that it was the British, and not the Ngoni before whom he was brought to trial.

Reactions to the verdict and sentence were understandably varied in detail, though almost universally anti-Ziehl. The Livingstonia mission periodical, *The Aurora* was critical of the verdict on some counts—thinking that it was the Ngoni who were provoked and not Ziehl.[58] It supported Fraser, saying that but for him Ziehl would not have escaped alive. It thought the verdict was lenient but on the whole praised the government for upholding justice.

Fraser himself thought that Ziehl had made a profit out of the affair—so many cattle had been returned to him—but also thought Daniel Nhlane and his friends were wrong to get involved in the way that they did.[59] Elmslie, while having reservations about Fraser's involvement, was more down to earth than perhaps any other European in his concern for the many Ngoni who had suffered loss through Ziehl's actions, and had not been compensated. He pressed Laws to speak to Sharpe about this matter, and also about the return of the forty guns confiscated by Ziehl from the Ngoni and handed to the collector at Fort Alston.[60]

The *Central African Times* (usually supportive of the European settler viewpoint) took what was perhaps a surprising line—not only expressing satisfaction that the case had got a fair hearing, but strongly supporting Fraser against Pearce's criticisms. 'Mr. Fraser only did what any right thinking man would have done in his place.'[61]

---

[56] *Central African Times*, 24 June 1899, 7.
[57] *UFCSMR*, April 1901, 258.
[58] *The Aurora*, June 1899, 17.
[59] Fraser, *Primitive People*, 109.
[60] Elmslie to Laws, 20 June 1899, Elmslie File, NLS.
[61] *Central African Times*, 24 June 1899, 6.

More interesting than any of these, of course, is the Ngoni view of the proceedings. Their initial reaction had been one of fear: the fear that 'Daniel has ruined our country',[62] i.e. that British justice would inevitably be pro-European, and that the affair would be used as an excuse to crush them, as their brothers at Mlangeni had been crushed. That the trial took place at all was probably something of a surprise to them; it certainly aroused widespread interest, and thousands of Ngoni arrived at Ekwendeni to hear the proceedings.[63]

Though it may seem surprising, the Ngoni were even impressed by the outcome, and forty years later, *inkosi yamakosi* M'mbelwa II in his evidence to the Bledisloe Commission cited the Ziehl case as one of the reasons why Chimtunga had eventually accepted British rule:

> This is one of the reasons that my father willingly placed himself under the Imperial government Rule because the Deputy Commissioner, Mr. Pearce, had displayed justice and shewed great protection by fining that European and making him pay all damages made to people.[64]

This is not to say that it made the Ngoni enthusiastic for British rule. It did not. Elmslie, for example, writing more than a year after the trial, commented to Laws that 'The Ngoni in many places have come and thanked us for keeping out the Administration'.[65] What it did, however, was to remove some of the dread which had previously characterised their attitude to the British administration.[66]

Besides, the Ngoni probably believed that in some measure they themselves had punished Ziehl. The nickname which they gave to him— *Kanjechi*—which is still vaguely remembered in parts of *uNgoni* to-day, might be translated, 'the one who was really beaten into shape'.[67] And what of the colonial government's attitude? Pearce, like many other Europeans—missionaries, planters and civil servants—believed that the trial provided the

---

[62] Fraser, *Autobiography*, 153.

[63] Pearce to Sharpe, 15 June 1899, FO 2/209, NAUK. An interesting photograph exists of paramount chief Chimtunga arriving to give evidence at the trial, through a guard of honour of colonial soldiers. I have reproduced it as Plate 11 in my *Christianity in Northern Malawi*. Unfortunately the quality is not very good.

[64] *Inkosi yamakosi* M'mbelwa's evidence to the Bledisloe Commission, quoted by Pachai, 'Ngoni Politics and Diplomacy in Malawi: 1849-1904' in Pachai (Ed.), *The Early History of Malawi*, London, 1972.

[65] Elmslie to Laws, 30 August 1900, Elmslie File, NLS.

[66] Note, for example, the remark made by one Ngoni witness when asked why he thought Ziehl was an agent of the government: 'because Ziehl and his men took things without paying for them', Pearce to Sharpe, 18 June 1899, FO 2/209, NAUK.

[67] J. L. Döhne, *A Zulu-Kafir Dictionary*, Cape Town, 1857, 156.

perfect opportunity for bringing *uNgoni* peacefully under British rule. He commented:

> There will be few opportunities more suitable than the present for opening out this large and thickly populated district, while the memories of the white man's trial and the event at Ekwendeni are impressed on their minds.[68]

Sharpe thought the case would hasten the time of the coming of the administration, but did not want to rush things, and preferred to leave the initiative to the Ngoni. In the event, it was not until 1904—thirteen years after the rest of what is now Malawi had come under colonial control, and with concessions not granted to any other indigenous group in the country—that the Ngoni agreed to come under British suzerainty.

Conclusion

By this period several new elements had been added to what had been the rather simplistic missionary attitude to Ngoni violence in the 1880s. The first was the coming of colonial government to Malawi in 1891. While, in general, the Scottish missionaries welcomed it, particularly as a safeguard against a possible Portuguese take-over, they were, nevertheless highly critical, at times, of colonial practice. The second was the appearance of growing numbers of what the missionaries regarded as disreputable Europeans in the area, so that they could no longer sustain any pretence that Europeans as such were morally superior to Africans. The third was that, as mission work became established among the Ngoni, and they began to respond to the Christian gospel, those missionaries working amongst them, began to develop a somewhat more sympathetic attitude towards the Ngoni in general, and to be willing to defend them against outsiders—whether African or European.

Yet in spite of all this, and of the considerable amount of European violence—both state-sponsored and individual—the stereotype of the 'wild Ngoni' was to persist well into the twentieth century.

---

[68] Pearce to Sharpe, 15 June 1899, FO 2/209, NAUK
.

Three-Way Struggle: Ngoni Identity, Scottish Missionaries and Colonial Government[1]

Introduction

Over the past forty years or so it has passed as historical orthodoxy to argue that Western Christian missionaries were closely tied to European colonial expansion into Africa, and approved of it wholeheartedly. While such a view clearly contains considerable elements of truth, and only a very few nineteenth century missionaries in Africa could be categorised as genuinely anti-colonial, it is nevertheless the case that the reality of the relationship between missionaries and colonial government was often much more complex than some historians have been prepared to admit.

In this paper I want to look at the complicated relations between the Ngoni people of northern Malawi, the Scottish missionaries of the Livingstonia mission of the Free Church of Scotland, and the British colonial authorities, in the period preceding the annexation of *uNgoni*[2] by the British in 1904.

British colonial authorities had first laid claim to the southern part of Malawi in 1890, and, in the following year a Protectorate had been proclaimed over the whole country. While theoretically, the British claimed the whole of Malawi from Nsanje to the Songwe river, the actual process of establishing effective control over the area was more gradual, and in several cases involved military action.[3] M'mbelwa's Ngoni had settled in the north of the country in 1855—predominantly in what is now Mzimba district—after a migration of thirty-five years from their original home near Lake St. Lucia in what is now KwaZulu-Natal.[4] In the 1880s and 1890s they had gradually come under the influence of the Livingstonia mission, and that,

---

[1] An earlier version of this paper was presented at an international conference on 'Christian Missions from the Eighteenth to the Twentieth Centuries' held in Moscow, from 16-18 May 1995, organised by the Institute of Universal History of the Russian Academy of Science and the Centre for the Study of Christianity in the Non-Western World, University of Edinburgh.
[2] Throughout I prefer the Ngoni term '*uNgoni*' as the name for the country, rather than the English term 'Ngoniland', used in many older historical accounts.
[3] For example, against the slave trader Mlozi, near Karonga in 1887, and chief Mwase Kasungu in 1896.
[4] See chapter one, 'Ngoni Origins' of my book, *Christianity in Northern Malawi,* Leiden, 1995.

together with other social and economic changes going on around them, had led to a gradual (and in many cases, reluctant) abandonment of their traditional way of life, involving raiding other surrounding groups for food and captives.

By 1900, M'mbelwa's Ngoni had seen all the other Ngoni groups around them picked off one by one by the British, and subjugated by force. By 1897 the administration had *Bomas* at both Mvera and Domwe, among Chiwere's and Gomani's Ngoni,[5] and when, in January 1898, Mpezeni's armies (in what is now the Chipata district of Eastern Zambia) were crushed by a British force under Captain Brake, which included artillery and Maxim guns,[6] the newly elected paramount of the northern Ngoni, Chimtunga Jere found himself the only remaining Ngoni chief not under direct colonial control.

News of Mpezeni's defeat was not long in reaching M'mbelwa's Ngoni. Mpezeni sent messengers north, and their reports produced great uneasiness in *uNgoni* at the possibility of British intervention there. Describing this reaction about a year later, the Scottish missionary Donald Fraser wrote (with perhaps more insight than most of his missionary colleagues)

> Ever since the Mpezeni war the chiefs here have been in dread that the Administration would come here next. This was increased by the account which messengers, whom Mpezeni sent to his brothers here, gave of the cause of the war, of the seizing of cattle, of the killing of Singu and some *indunas*, and of the conduct of the North Charterland Police.[7]

It is clear from Fraser's description above, that it was not simply the defeat itself, but what the northern Ngoni perceived to be the nature of that defeat, which produced their dread of British intervention. They believed, with Mpezeni, that the administration had provoked the war; they regarded the confiscation of thousands of Mpezeni's cattle and the execution of Singu[8] as acts of extremism and sacrilege, and they were soon to have first hand experience themselves of the conduct of the North Charterland Police.[9]

It is probably true, as McCracken points out,[10] that after the Mpezeni war the will to resist by force had deserted M'mbelwa's Ngoni. Elmslie several

---

[5] K.M Phiri, 'Chewa History in Central Malawi and the Use of Oral Tradition, 1600-1920', University of Wisconsin-Madison, PhD thesis, 1975, 194.

[6] J. A. Barnes, *Politics in a Changing Society: a Political History of the Fort Jameson Ngoni*, London, 1954, 91.

[7] *Central African Times*, 15 April 1899; letter from Fraser concerning the Ziehl case, 5.

[8] Singu was a sub-chief of Nkosi Mpezeni.

[9] For a more detailed account of the Ziehl case, see the chapter 'Bloodthirsty Savages or Stout-Hearted Zulus' in this book.

[10] John McCracken, *Politics and Christianity in Malawi*, 111.

times makes the same point around this period.[11] What is not always appreciated is the genuine apprehension and dread with which many of the northern Ngoni viewed the possible arrival of the colonial administration.

What is apparent at this time is the split in the Ngoni nation between those seeking to uphold the old way of life based on military raiding, and those wanting to follow a way of life which took more account of the new external forces of wage labour, colonial presence, and mission influence. The former group was epitomised by *induna* Ng'onomo Makamu, and, to a lesser extent, by *inkosi* Mpherembe; the latter by the younger leaders Johane and Amos Jere at Ekwendeni, and the Nhlane brothers at Hoho.

In 1896 Ng'onomo became involved in a dangerous confrontation with British authorities when he gave shelter to, and refused to surrender Chibisa, a headman of Mwase Kasungu, who had fought against the British and then fled north to uNgoni.[12] Ng'onomo's reluctance to hand over the fugitive headman Chibisa was not simply the stubbornness of an old man; it was a reluctance to submit to a new way of life in which he had no stake—a new set of values to which he owed no allegiance. The raiding to which he stubbornly clung must be seen not merely as a military, but also as an economic activity. In 1889 Elmslie had written of the Ngoni, 'They are mad for war just now as no trade has been here since the Karonga war began'.[13] However, the possibility of acquiring wealth by raiding became more and more remote as the 1890s wore on. The effective colonial occupation of much the northern region of Malawi, with the opening of *Bomas* at Deep Bay [Chilumba] and Nkhata Bay in 1893 and 1897 greatly restricted the areas into which the Ngoni could freely raid.[14] In 1896 Harry Johnston made 'no raiding' a provision of his offer to the Ngoni that as long as they did not cause the administration any expense they would be left in peace and not taxed.[15]

Alternative forms of economic activity such as education (in the hope of later being employed by the mission), or wage labour at Deep Bay or further afield, were beginning to attract growing numbers of Ngoni youths from the early 1890s onwards.

---

[11] Elmslie to Smith, 9 April 1896, Ms. 7879, and 4 March 1898, Ms. 7881; Elmslie to Laws, 11 November 1902, Elmslie File; all refs. NLS.

[12] For a more detailed account of the Chibisa affair, see Thompson, *Christianity in Northern Malawi*, 105-06.

[13] Elmslie to Laws, 10 October 1889, Ms. 7892, NLS.

[14] Richard Crawshay, 'A Journey in the Angoni Country' in *The Geographical Journal*, Vol. III, 1894, 59-60; and C.A. Cardew, 'Nyasaland in 1894-5' in *The Nyasaland Journal*, 1(1), January 1948, 52.

[15] Elmslie to Laws, 11 April 1896, Elmslie File, NLS.

Finally, though it was by no means the only factor which led to the decline of raiding, the presence and influence of the Livingstonia mission, and of the youthful band of committed Ngoni Christians was by the mid-1890s exerting a powerful influence against any continuance of large-scale raiding.

Both the influences of outside events, and the gradual decline of raiding as a viable way of life, were forcing the Ngoni into some sort of accommodation with the administration. The outworking of this process can be seen both in the Chibisa affair, and more widely. The letter which several Ngoni chiefs sent to Swann during the Chibisa affair, expressing willingness to be friendly with the British,[16] was not so much an indication of their desire for friendship, as of their fear of British enmity. Once the crisis had passed, and the risk of British intervention had receded, several of those who had signed the letters of friendship agreed to join Mpezeni in a joint army to try to oust the British from Fort Alston.[17] To some extent this was the same pattern which was to emerge in 1904 and immediately afterwards, when acceptance of annexation was too easily equated—by missionaries and government officials alike—with enthusiasm for British rule.

Missionary Attitudes towards Colonial Government in the 1890s

Several writers, including myself, have pointed out the differing attitudes of Livingstonia missionaries towards the Ngoni, emphasizing that those working in marginal areas were much less likely to be sympathetic to the Ngoni than those working within *uNgoni* itself.[18] Of those missionaries working within *uNgoni*, Elmslie was by far the most active and involved politically (at least until the arrival of Fraser, and his own departure on furlough in 1897) and it is from a study of his attitudes that the nature of the mission's impact in the 1890s will be most apparent.

Throughout the 1890s three elements are clear in Elmslie's thinking on the relationship of Ngoni, mission and colonial government. These are, first, the general desirability of British rule for the Ngoni; secondly, the protection of the Ngoni against what he saw as unjust British interference in specific circumstances; and thirdly, a deep-seated suspicion of H.H. Johnston, the first colonial Commissioner of Malawi, and a belief that Johnston was scheming to overcome M'mbelwa's Ngoni by force.

---

[16] *Ibid.,* 11 April 1896.

[17] *Ibid.,* 20 July 1896.

[18] See, for example, John McCracken, *Politics*, 171-73.

Elmslie's uneasiness about the mission becoming an arm of the colonial government in its relations with the Ngoni is apparent as early as 1889 when he asked Robert Laws, the leader of the mission, for his views on whether or not the mission should introduce H.H. Johnston to the Ngoni.[19] (In the event, Johnston appears not to have visited them.) After initial misgivings at this period about the Ngoni signing a treaty with the British, which he told Laws he would advise them against doing,[20] Elmslie by the mid-1890s had become firmly convinced of the desirability of British control. His views are neatly summed up in a letter he wrote to Laws in August 1895:

> As for Ngoniland and the Government I believe it would be for the good of the people and good for us in view of changes inevitably coming if the country were under the Government rather than under the B.S.A. Co. As to helping the Government further than neutrality, that may or may not be wise for us. There are dangers in taking part, even by countenancing arrangements, and there might be worse dangers in holding aloof. I should like to see the treaty before committing myself, and I should also want to know how far, if assistance were given, our opinion would rule the *modus operandi*... But I do not like the idea of being mixed up with Government business.[21]

By 1897 he was writing that 'the sooner the country is under British rule the better for all',[22] but a few months earlier, when asked by Johnston to call a meeting of the Ngoni, he had complained to George Smith, Secretary of the Foreign Mission Committee in Scotland that he had no wish to do the government's work for them.[23]

This unwillingness to interfere on behalf of the British administration arose partly from his fear that if the mission encouraged the Ngoni to sign a treaty which later turned out to be unpopular, then the Ngoni would blame the missionaries, and their popularity and influence would consequently suffer.[24] On the other hand, a strong element in his desire for neutrality was undoubtedly his eagerness to protect the Ngoni from what he regarded as specific incidents of unjust British treatment: his determination not to allow the Ngoni to be badgered.

This attitude is particularly noticeable during the Chibisa affair, and brought him into temporary disagreement with Dr. Laws who wanted him to

---

[19] Elmslie to Laws, 21 October 1889, Ms. 7892, NLS.

[20] *Ibid.*, 23 September 1889.

[21] Elmslie to Laws, 13 August 1895, Elmslie File, NLS.

[22] *Ibid.,* 9 March 1897.

[23] Elmslie to Smith, 24 June 1896, Ms. 7879, NLS.

[24] *Ibid.,* 9 April 1896.

take a more pro-British line with the Ngoni; but Elmslie stood firm, refusing to advise the Ngoni to request British protection.

> Dr. Laws urges our getting the Ngoni to take time by the forelock and voluntarily hand over their country to the British. I agree it will come to British rule very soon but I am not anxious to negotiate that, as when taxes are put on there may be some dissatisfaction and we would be blamed; besides, the Ngoni ought not to make themselves cheap... I am as anxious as he [H.H. Johnston] to see the Ngoni under his rule, and it may be accomplished without bloodshed (except the settling of Ng'onomo which I see entails war) provided he is patient, and I will render him all the assistance I can, but I will not agree to countenance anything in him of a terrifying nature.[25]

Underlying all Elmslie's attitudes however, was a deep-seated distrust of H.H. Johnston, which can be traced as far back as 1889, but which becomes more distinct and vociferous during late 1890 and early 1891, when both Johnston and Elmslie were on leave in Britain. Elmslie took particular objection to Johnston's scheme for an Anglo-Arab alliance against the Ngoni, outlined in his article in the *Fortnightly Review*,[26] and prepared a written statement for the Livingstonia committee in which he criticised Johnston's conduct of the Arab war, and his treaty with the Jumbe of Nkhotakota.[27]

Elmslie was convinced that Johnston was looking for an excuse to make war on the northern Ngoni, and this view seems to have been shared, at least partly, by Laws, who reported that after the defeat of the slave trader Mlozi at Karonga Johnston deliberately ordered those transporting the cattle and spoils south, to go through *uNgoni* in the hope of provoking the Ngoni to steal them—thus providing a cause for war. According to Laws, the porters (perhaps fearful for their own safety) had taken the lakeshore route instead.[28] Though the accuracy of this story is uncertain, it was eagerly believed by Elmslie, and provided, in his view, a further justification for his beliefs about Johnston's intentions.

During the Chibisa affair, Elmslie was convinced that Swann was acting on instructions from Johnston to foment trouble, and claimed that his advice to the chiefs to send letters to Swann proclaiming their desire for friendship with the British had pre-empted any military action on Johnston's part.

---

[25] *Ibid.*

[26] H.H. Johnston, 'The Development of Tropical Africa under British Auspices', in *The Fortnightly Review*, 1 November 1890, 684-706.

[27] Elmslie to Laws, 12 April 1891, Ms. 7895, NLS.

[28] Elmslie to Smith, 9 April 1896, Ms. 7879, NLS.

In 1897, while Johnston was away from Malawi, Elmslie believed that his successor 'Sharpe has distinct instructions not to touch the Ngoni in any way. It is the next card that Sir Harry wants to play himself.' At the time it was thought possible that Johnston might return to Malawi, though, according to Baker he had hinted in private correspondence that he did not want to come back. If this is the case Elmslie's views must be regarded as somewhat neurotic, though his judgment that 'it will be to the credit of the Mission if they voluntarily submit, but to his fame if he subdues them by war' may not only be accurate, but may well provide an important clue to the motivation of both Johnston and Elmslie in their relations with the Ngoni at this period. In any case, the departure of both Johnston and Elmslie on leave in 1897, their respective replacement by Sharpe and Fraser, and the election of a new Ngoni paramount chief, meant that control of the situation was passing into new hands.

Fraser's attitudes towards the Ngoni and the colonial government, once they had become clear, did not differ essentially from those of Elmslie. He had no direct experience of Sir Harry Johnston, and the Livingstonia missionaries in general got on much better with Alfred Sharpe; nevertheless, like Elmslie, Fraser believed both that the Ngoni would be better off under British rule, and that the missionaries should protect them against unwarranted outside interference.

In Fraser's first three year tour of duty, while his views were still somewhat fluid, there were some apparent contradictions in his actions. In some respects he seemed to be more pro-British than Elmslie—in 1898 encouraging the Ngoni chiefs to invite Britain to come in; in other respects more pro-Ngoni—possibly encouraging *inkosi* Mtwalo to collect his own taxes and set up his own police force. What is clear, is that, while he tried to avoid assuming the position of a civil magistrate, he nevertheless involved himself in a very direct way in several affairs where Ngoni interests were at stake. Foremost among these was the Ziehl case of 1899, when a European adventurer entered *uNgoni* to buy cattle, and left behind him a trail of death, destruction and rape.[29] The missionaries, especially Fraser, took a very strong line in supporting the Ngoni and insisting to the colonial authorities that Ziehl must be brought to trial. He was, in fact, tried, and found guilty of several charges. The whole incident did, however, lead the colonial authorities to consider more actively annexing *uNgoni* more formally into the British colonial orbit.

---

[29] This is dealt with in detail in the chapter: 'Bloodthirsty Savages or Stout-Hearted Zulus'.

The Coming of Colonial Government

Sharpe's eventual decision not to annex *uNgoni* immediately after the Ziehl case was based, not on any ultimate reluctance to take the step, but on the assessment that it would be more prudent 'to leave it to be proposed by the Angoni themselves, as I feel sure they will do so before long'.[30] As it turned out Sharpe's judgment was wrong. More than five years were to separate the Ziehl case and British annexation of *uNgoni*, and when the latter event took place in September 1904 the initiative was to come, not from the Ngoni, but from the colonial administration itself, and, to a lesser extent, from the mission.

Elmslie, by now back in Malawi, regretted the delay, feeling that Sharpe had made a mistake in not annexing the area before he left on leave in 1900.[31] He realised that Ngoni support for such a move was minimal, and probably decreasing. The Ngoni valued their independence more highly than perhaps the colonial authorities realised, and while the Ziehl case had undoubtedly reduced Ngoni fears about government intentions, it had also re-enforced their belief that they could look after themselves. So too had the attitude of Fraser in 1899 and early 1900.

Some time in 1899, probably as a result of the Ziehl case, Fraser encouraged Mtwalo at Ekwendeni to establish his own hut tax and raise his own police force.[32] This move was strongly opposed by Elmslie, who later wrote to Laws, 'I cannot but regret Mr. Fraser's ill-considered attempt to bolster up their independence and it will react on our work as we shall see.'[33] Nevertheless, Fraser carried a letter from the Ngoni chiefs to Sharpe[34] (probably as he went south on his way home to Scotland early in 1900) in which they claimed the right, not only to collect taxes, but also to pursue runaway *abafo* into territories administered by the British. The administration seemed to have denied this right, but this attitude only caused resentment among the Ngoni chiefs, without effectively reducing their power.

The Ngoni chiefs, in effect, were trying to play the mission off against the administration, claiming in their letter to Sharpe, 'We are for the Mission and not the Boma'.[35] They probably realised by this stage that their

---

[30] Sharpe to Foreign Office, 16th June 1899, FO2/209, National Archives (UK).

[31] Elmslie to Laws, 30th August 1900, Elmslie File, NLS.

[32] Fraser, 'Zulu', 74.

[33] Elmslie to Laws, 30th August 1900, Elmslie File, NLS.

[34] *Ibid.*, 5th January 1902.

[35] *Ibid.*

continued existence as a powerful people depended on coming to terms with one of the outside groups who were influencing the area,[36] and judged that an alliance with the mission would allow them greater scope than submission to the colonial administration. In thinking this way, of course, they misjudged the political inclinations of most missionaries, who actually favoured annexation; but certainly the relationship they built up with the mission in this period was looked upon with envy by other Ngoni groups elsewhere in Malawi.

After a period of relative quiet, however, a series of disputes broke out between the Ngoni and the administration in late 1902 and early 1903. These disputes highlighted both the conflicting claims to authority in the areas surrounding *uNgoni* itself, and the continuing ambiguity of the missionary position. At least three incidents took place, two of them described by Elmslie as raids[37]—one to the foothills of the Nyika, and another to Kaning'ina on the borders between Ngoni and Tonga territory. In fact, they were not raids in the old sense, but something more akin to family feuds, as was the third disturbance—a case of revenge murder in which the alleged murderer's whole family were killed.

Though Knipe (the prosecutor in the Ziehl case, and now Collector at Nkhata Bay) left the murder case in Mtwalo's hands, *Inkosi yaMakosi* Chimtunga was held responsible for the two 'raids' and reported to Zomba. Some months later Chimtunga and the other chiefs were fined six cows each, and ordered to deliver up the raiders at Nkhata Bay to be punished by Knipe. Elmslie reacted vigorously. Though he himself thought the Ngoni were wrong, he objected to the lack of a proper judicial procedure:

> Chimtunga could not understand the case, and I informed Mr. Knipe of that and proposed that he should in the first instant make a charge and refrain from fining and punishing until there was a trial, as obviously, they had heard only one side… I then protested in strong and plain terms that the infliction of a fine on the chiefs while as yet no one for whom they were responsible had been lawfully tried and convicted of an offence was subversive of justice, and contrary to all law… Knipe then wrote that he would take the responsibility of leaving over the fine till after the trial.[38]

It was at this point that the colonial administration began to think seriously about annexing *uNgoni*—with Knipe making plans to choose a site for a

---

[36] In a sense, of course, one might argue that the establishment of such external alliances had been the Ngoni strategy from soon after the mission had arrived among them more than twenty years previously.
[37] Elmslie to Laws, November and 8th December 1902, Elmslie File, NLS.
[38] *Ibid.,* 18th April 1903.

Boma, and Sharpe explaining that the inability of the Ngoni chiefs to control their own subjects, and the increase in quarrels between the Ngoni and other tribes had made it

> evident during the past year [1903-04] that the time had come for the Protectorate Administration to finally place Mombera's Angoniland in the same position as all other districts in the Protectorate.[39]

Before that happened, however, there was to be one final serious dispute between the Ngoni and the administration—this time involving the intrusion of the colonial authorities into *uNgoni.*

In 1904 a group of colonial policemen entered *uNgoni* from the east, began collecting hut tax, giving inadequate receipts to those who paid, and burning the huts of those who didn't.[40] This was not a case of straying a mile or two across the boundary of *uNgoni*—generally accepted as the line of the Vipya hills which forms the watershed between the Kasitu/South Rukuru and the lake—but of penetrating more than thirty miles—right across Ngoni territory. Fraser was touring with his wife in the area at the time, and he intervened with the police and sent them back to Nkhata Bay with a letter for Pickford, the new Collector there. He explained that he had assured the Ngoni that the *Boma* would make good any damage caused by the police.

Pickford apparently resented what he saw as Fraser's interference, and after the matter had been reported to Zomba, an enquiry was ordered. Fraser attended this, together with *inkosi* Mzukuzuku. The police accused Fraser of inciting the people to murder them, defying the government, and trying to rouse the Ngoni to rebel. From Fraser's point of view the enquiry was inconclusive and unsatisfactory. Though it produced a government apology for the unauthorised intrusion,[41] it also resulted in a letter from Sharpe to Laws expressing criticism of Fraser's attitude to the government. From the Ngoni point of view, however, the outcome was much more serious: it provided the final excuse for the annexation of *uNgoni* by the British.

In outlining later in the year the events which led to annexation Sharpe pointed out that Johnston had promised the Ngoni chiefs

> That as long as they were able to administer their internal affairs without causing trouble to outsiders, and also kept their people under such control as would prevent raids on tax-paying natives in the Protectorate, they would be

---

[39] Sharpe to Colonial Office, 14th October 1904, 'Visit to Lake Nyasa Districts', paragraph 9, CO 525/3, NAUK.

[40] The following account is based on Agnes Fraser, *Donald Fraser*, 105-108, unless otherwise stated.

[41] Fraser, *Primitive People*, 240.

subject neither to taxation nor would British Officials be sent to administer their internal affairs.[42]

Sharpe went on to point out that the power of the Ngoni chiefs had been decreasing over the past few years, and that as they were no longer able to comply with these conditions, the time had come to annex *uNgoni*.

Both Elmslie and Fraser wrote articles describing the annexation, and explaining the background to it. Elmslie stressed that *uNgoni* had become a refuge for evil-doers from outside, fleeing from government justice. He pointed out that for several years the mission had been urging the government to annex the area, but that even up until 1903 Sharpe was unwilling to do so, 'without an armed force able to cope with eventualities'.[43]

Fraser stressed the unity of the tribe, which he claimed was beginning to break down with the deaths of the old chiefs, and the scattering of the tribe into new areas.[44] Villagers were raiding those against whom they had a grievance, and others, dissatisfied with a chief's judgment, were taking their cases to the nearest *Boma*. In Fraser's view, the confusion thus arising made the time ripe for annexation.[45]

While all these opinions doubtless contain aspects of the truth, it is ironical that the two major incidents which awakened Europeans to the need for British control of *uNgoni* were both cases of outsiders intruding into the area in a violent and illegal manner.[46]

The summons to meet Sharpe in *indaba* at Ekwendeni was not greeted by the Ngoni with any great enthusiasm. Indeed, the way in which it was issued greatly disturbed Chimtunga.[47] The missionaries, on the other hand, were unanimous in thinking that the annexation was desirable, though they had two particular concerns about the way it should be carried out. The first, with which Laws was principally concerned, was that the mission should not be directly involved in the negotiations—that they should be seen by the Ngoni to be separate from the administration.[48] The second, which concerned the missionaries working in *uNgoni* was, as Fraser put it, 'to get as good terms

---

[42] Sharpe to CO, 14th October 1904, CO 525/3, NAUK.

[43] *UFCSMR*, February 1905, 74-75.

[44] Fraser himself had taken part in 1902 in the migration of Mzukuzuku's people from near Hora mountain to the area of the Lwasozi river—leading to the opening of Loudon mission station.

[45] *Ibid.,* January 1905, 25-26.

[46] The Ziehl case of 1899, and the hut tax intrusion of 1904.

[47] Agnes Fraser, *Donald Fraser*, 108.

[48] W.P. Livingstone, *Laws*, 315.

of annexation as possible'.[49] That the two should be to some extent contradictory, was the inevitable outcome of the position of intermediaries which the missionaries had adopted over the years. The result was that the missionaries carried out informal talks with Sharpe before the *indaba*, but were mere spectators during the actual negotiations with the Ngoni.

This took place at Ekwendeni on the afternoon of Friday 2nd September 1904.[50] Sharpe explained to the Ngoni that they had spread out well beyond the limits of what had been their area of jurisdiction when H.H. Johnston had made his promise of non-interference; they must, therefore, return to that restricted area, or come under British jurisdiction.

The Ngoni chiefs accepted the inevitability of annexation. Their recent migrations had been made for mainly agricultural reasons and could not easily be reversed. Nevertheless, they had several problems which they wanted to discuss. One was the possibility of further migration as land became exhausted; another was the problem of how to prevent dissatisfied litigants playing off one chief against another; a third was a demand for an assurance that they would have the right to hunt game in particular areas.[51] Sharpe's assurance that the government had no intention of taking their cattle from them was obviously a response to a deep-seated Ngoni fear, which had been particularly strong since the Mpezeni war.

In his report on the *indaba* Sharpe listed nine terms which were agreed between the Ngoni and himself. These were, that a government official should be placed in *uNgoni*; that the Ngoni should be subject to the administration; that hut tax should not begin until January 1906; that the government would wipe the slate clean as far as previous disputes involving the Ngoni were concerned; that as far as possible the local police force should be made up of the Ngoni themselves; that six Ngoni chiefs would receive annual subsidies; that the Ngoni could hunt within the bend of the Rukuru river; that a new country would be found for those who needed to migrate, and that the people would be kept as far as possible with their old chiefs.

The occasion ended with the giving of thanks and traditional dancing, and both the missionaries and the colonial authorities expressed themselves highly satisfied with the outcome. But what of the Ngoni attitude to the settlement? Did they regard it with the same enthusiasm?

---

[49] Agnes Fraser, *Donald Fraser*, 108.
[50] The following account is based on Sharpe to CO, 14th October 1904, CO 525/3, NAUK, unless otherwise stated.
[51] *UFCSMR*, January 1905, 26.

Ngoni Attitudes to Annexation

European accounts of the annexation would seem to indicate that the Ngoni reaction was one of willing acceptance—if not, indeed, of enthusiasm. Sharpe wrote that the chiefs 'without hesitation accepted the new condition of affairs',[52] while Fraser commented that Sharpe's proposals 'were almost immediately accepted, and with much heartiness'.[53] A more accurate understanding of Ngoni attitudes may be arrived at by considering why the Ngoni accepted the proposals at all, and examining briefly their actions in the period immediately following annexation.

Pachai suggests four factors which led the northern Ngoni to accept colonial rule.[54] These were the Ziehl case, the rinderpest epidemic of 1893, the incompetent rule of Chimtunga, and the 1904 tax-collecting incident. It has already been pointed out that the main impact of the Ziehl case was in reducing fears of a colonial take-over, and to this extent it was of considerable importance as a factor making annexation more likely in the long-run. On the other hand, there was a sense in which the Ziehl case encouraged the Ngoni in their belief that they were able to deal with such intrusions themselves. While the rinderpest epidemic undoubtedly had a serious impact at the time, the Ngoni herds had recovered well before 1904, and it may be doubted whether it had any direct impact on the coming of colonial government. What is certainly true (and it may be that this is what Pachai implies) is that the recovery of Ngoni herds after 1893, actually led to an increased influx of people such as Ziehl, seeking to buy cattle, and that this influx inevitably led to more interaction with the colonial authorities. The disillusionment of other Ngoni chiefs with Chimtunga (he was never, for example, given the honorary title M'mbelwa) may have been a factor which made them more willing to accept colonial rule—or rather, to seek colonial backing for their own position as chiefs; while the 1904 tax-collecting incident had more effect on the attitudes of the administration than those of the Ngoni.

To Pachai's points may be added the following. First, the Ngoni had no real alternative. Sharpe's proposals on 2nd September, though open to discussion, and possible amendment, were not open to rejection. It was for this reason that he had presented the Ngoni with the choice of accepting colonial rule or returning to their former boundaries; the latter was not a

---

[52] Sharpe to CO, 14th October 1904.

[53] *UFCSMR*, January 1905, 25.

[54] Bridglal Pachai, 'Ngoni Politics and Diplomacy in Malawi: 1849-1904' in Pachai (ed.), *The Early History of Malawi*.

realistic option; there was, in effect, no choice at all. The only real alternative would have been military revolt, and that had ceased to be a realistic possibility several years previously.

Secondly, the Ngoni may have accepted annexation without complaint, on the mistaken assumption that they were being offered much more than they actually were. *Inkosi yamakosi* M'mbelwa II in his evidence to the Bledisloe Commission in the 1930s argued that his father Chimtunga agreed to annexation because the government had on several earlier occasions

> promised him that his kingdom will be as that of Khama and the Prince of Zanzibar, and that no European will have power over his country and over him, also that Her Majesty Queen Victoria will send a consul to help him and to strengthen his power and that his people will pay taxes to him and not to Her Majesty the Queen.[55]

Whether these promises were, in fact, made is now very difficult to establish, though Fraser reports Sharpe as telling the Ngoni on 2nd September of his proposal to put a government official among them, who would strengthen their hands to govern the people'.[56] The most likely explanation is that the Ngoni read into Sharpe's remarks more than he intended, and were later disillusioned with the reality of colonial government.

Thirdly, the continuous influence of the mission, which, while attempting to protect Ngoni interests against outside interference, nevertheless encouraged the Ngoni in the belief that colonial government would be to their ultimate advantage, must have had a considerable influence, not only on Ngoni teachers such as Mawelera Tembo and Daniel Nhlane, but also on the chiefs themselves, all of whom were in regular contact with the missionaries.

Finally, the gradual intrusion of a wage economy into the life of the Ngoni helped to undermine the traditional structures of the state and to ensure, even before 1904, their *de facto* inclusion in the economic orbit of the Protectorate. This very weakening of traditional power structures may, paradoxically, have persuaded the chiefs that the acceptance of and alliance with colonial government would be one way of preserving their own chiefly authority.

Whatever the precise importance of each of these points, it seems clear that the initial Ngoni reaction to colonial government was one of reluctant acceptance of the inevitable, rather than enthusiastic support for the

---

[55] *Inkosi* M'mbelwa's evidence to Bledisloe Commission, quoted in Pachai, 'Ngoni Politics', 206.
[56] *UFCSMR*, January 1905, 25.

desirable. This was especially true at village level, where some people sent their cattle to other parts of the country, fearing the government intended to rob them, and others refused to supply H.C. Macdonald, whom Sharpe had appointed as Resident, with labourers, carriers, or food for sale. Chimtunga at first refused even to see Macdonald, or to send carriers or men for police work, and though the situation improved significantly in the next few years,[57] the seeds of discontent remained—ready to break forth again in 1915, during the First World War.[58]

To conclude, can we draw any conclusions from this case study about the interaction of Ngoni, missionaries and colonial authorities in Malawi at the beginning of the twentieth century? First, British missionaries working in areas under the colonial control of the British, were generally in favour of the principle of British colonial control. Certainly, in the Malawi context, they much preferred it to the possibility of Portuguese or German control.

Secondly, on the other hand, they often opposed particular colonial policies of the colonial government, which they regarded as unjust to the people amongst whom they were working. The Scottish missionaries in general had a very touchy relationship with Harry Johnston; and while it was mainly the Blantyre missionaries in the south of the country whom he regarded as 'Her Majesty's Official Opposition', the Livingstonia missionaries too were prepared to oppose him (and later Sharpe) when they felt African interests were being threatened.

Thirdly, the missionaries were often keen to establish their separate identity from the colonial authorities, by distinguishing their own policies, agendas and priorities from those of the government.

Fourthly, local peoples, on the whole, did not make such a clear-cut distinction between the missionaries and the colonial government. They tended to link the two groups together as 'wazungu', and to believe that their interests, if not identical, were certainly similar.

Fifthly, on the other hand, African awareness that there were differences of emphasis and interest between different groups of Europeans, encouraged them to exploit these differences when they could be found. It was not only the colonial authorities who used the tactic of 'divide and rule'!

Sixthly, it therefore follows that groups such as the Ngoni ought not to be regarded by historians merely as helpless objects tossed about on a sea of colonial policy-making, but rather, to some extent at least, as interest groups

---

[57] *BCA Protectorate, Report for 1905-06*, 22.
[58] At that time Chimtunga again refused to provide carriers or food to help with the war effort, and, as a result was arrested, deposed, and exiled to Chiromo, in the extreme south of Malawi.

able to exercise political skill in trying to control the situation to achieve their own particular strategic ends.

Seventhly, and finally, the methods of nineteenth and early twentieth century historiography have meant that the records remaining for us are heavily biased in favour of what might be called 'the European explanation' of the events being analysed. It is imperative that we do everything we can to recover the African view of such events—whether oral or written.

We may conclude with one small example of this. The stereotype of 'the wild Ngoni' is well-known, and still trotted out even today; but when we turn to Yesaya Chibambo's account of the annexation we get a very different picture. The Ngoni remain very proud of their military heritage, of course, as can be seen whenever a group of *ngoma* dancers gather to perform. When Chibambo came to write about the events of September 1904, however, it was not the military might of the Ngoni which he chose to highlight. Instead, in his 'Makani gha waNgoni' — later published in English as *My Ngoni of Nyasaland*[59]—he indicated that Ngoni pride on that day lay in an entirely different direction. On the penultimate page of the account occurs this passage:

> Para Boma likanjira mu *uNgoni* pa 1904 kuti donto limoza la ndopa likatirikapo cara; ndipo nkongono ya wayeni yirive kutayapo wonga wake kutereska fuko litu; nga ndi umo kuli kucitikira mu vyaru vinyake. Bwana Mkubwa Sir Alfred Sharpe, wakiza yeka na muwoli wake kwambura msirikari wa nkondo, ndipo pa September 2, iyo na waNgoni wakazomerezgana kuti Boma liwenge mu *uNgoni*.[60]

> When the government entered Ngoniland in 1904 not a drop of blood was shed, as was done in some other parts of the land. The Governor, Sir Alfred Sharpe, came alone with his wife and with no armed force, and on 2nd September he and the Ngoni agreed that the Government be established in Ngoniland.[61]

The interplay of ideas in this passage is fascinating. M'mbelwa's Ngoni had seen all their neighbours picked off one by one by the British colonial authorities, and subjugated by force. For Chibambo it was a source of great pride that (from his perspective) the northern Ngoni had been strong enough to resist this fate. At the same time, once the time of annexation could no longer be delayed, it was significant, not only that it was achieved 'without a

---

[59] 'Makani gha waNgoni' in *Midauko*, Livingstonis Synod, Blantyre, 1965; *My Ngoni of Nyasaland*, edited by Charles Stuart, (Africa's Own Library, No. 3), Heinemann, London, 1940.

[60] 'Makani gha waNgoni', 85.

[61] *My Ngoni of Nyasaland*, 59; Charles Stuart's translation.

single drop of blood being spilt', but also that Sharpe came to the *indaba*, not with a contingent of armed soldiers, but with his wife. Here Chibambo is highlighting Ngoni trustworthiness—a quality in which they took great pride. The annexation of 1904 was a traumatic event for the Ngoni, and it was important that they could interpret it in a way which allowed them to retain some of their self-esteem. The credit that this was enabled to happen, must, I think, be shared by all three parties involved. The Scottish missionaries patiently worked over a number of years to ensure that the Ngoni were willing to consider the issue, and that the colonial authorities did not act prematurely; the colonial authorities, for their part, while they had brutally suppressed other Ngoni groups, were prepared to negotiate, rather than fight, with M'mbelwa's Ngoni; and the Ngoni themselves, though having severe reservations about the annexation, were prepared to accept the inevitable, rather than engage in a last, futile gesture of military might. It had, indeed, been a three-way struggle; but one from which all three parties emerged with some degree of credit.

'Brave and Honourable Gentlemen': Scottish Missionary Attitudes to African Culture and Religion

Almost exactly a hundred years ago[1] a young Scottish missionary, just home after having completed his first tour of duty in Africa, rose to address the Philosophical Society of Glasgow. His chosen topic was 'the Zulu of Nyasaland: their Manners and Customs'[2] and his talk— ranging across history, linguistics, anthropology and religion —consisted of a slightly strange mixture of Christian confidence on the one hand, and empathy with the people about whom he was speaking on the other.

The missionary was Donald Fraser, who was to go on to become one of the most prolific of Scottish missionaries to what is now Malawi to appear in print. During the next twenty-five years he published six books, and scores of articles in a wide variety of journals and newspapers. By the middle of the 1920s he had become an internationally respected missionary statesman, and his views on things African were influential—both in Scotland, and in the worldwide missionary community. His lecture to the Philosophical Society of Glasgow is important, in that it represents the first serious attempt by Fraser to grapple with the issues of how western Christianity was to relate to African culture and religion: an issue which was, of course, particularly sensitive in the pioneer period when missionaries (and to a limited extent local Christians) were beginning to lay down laws and customs of church discipline—deciding which aspects of local culture were acceptable, and which were not.

Like many of his generation, Fraser was a product of the Student Volunteer Movement, with its Watchword 'The Evangelisation of the World in this Generation'.[3] It therefore goes without saying that his commitment to, and confidence in the eventual triumph of Christianity were strong. In some cases, such commitment could lead to an extremely negative attitude to African traditional culture and religion. In the case of Fraser (and several of

---

[1] This paper was first given at a 'Currents in World Christianity' conference in Edinburgh in 2001. It is published here for the first time.

[2] Donald Fraser, 'The Zulu of Nyasaland: their Manners and Customs' in *Proceedings of the Philosophical Society of Glasgow*, Vol. Xxxii, 1900-1901, 60-75.

[3] For a more detailed account of Fraser's early life, see T. Jack Thompson, *Christianity in Northern Malawi*, 72-82.

his Scottish colleagues in Malawi), however, the attitude was much more ambivalent.

Yet what is surprising in Fraser's lecture, is the comparative lack of condemnatory language—even about customs of which the mission certainly disapproved, such as polygamy, and the widespread praise, verging on enthusiasm, for may aspects of Ngoni culture and religion. 'Our Ngoni' says Fraser, 'came to Nyasaland as a moral blessing'. 'The aristocratic Ngoni is a gentleman through and through' continues Fraser, 'His word is absolute. When he gives a promise you may fearlessly rely on it. He does not steal, nor does he intrude on your privacy.'[4] It has to be said here, that this view appears to be in direct contradiction to that of Fraser's colleague Elmslie. One explanation of this is that both missionaries contrasted the behaviour of the 'pure' Ngoni (what I call the *abaZansi*[5]) with that of their domestic slaves whom they had acquired during their long migration from the south.

Fraser calls the Ngoma dance 'prettiest and most delightful',[6] though there were other dances of which he was much less enthusiastic. With regard to religion he comments that he doesn't intend to say much, as the topic needs long and careful investigation. This in itself is a healthy attitude, not always found among all of his colleagues. What he does have to say about Ngoni religion is low-key and largely descriptive, including reference to reverence for the ancestral spirits, and the sacrificing of cattle to the ancestors. He even comments enthusiastically, 'Like other children of nature, there are men and women in the tribe who seem to have a wonderful gift of second sight'.[7]

Fraser does take it for granted that Christianity will eventually triumph over Ngoni traditional religion. What is distinctive in his attitude—and this was to remain the case throughout his missionary career—is his strong concern that the Christianity which the Ngoni adopted should be built on, rather than merely replacing, what the Ngoni referred to as *ubuNgoni* ('Ngoniness' or 'the essence of being Ngoni'). This is most forcefully expressed at the end of his lecture when he argues:

> Yet it would be a pity if with this inrush of new life the old tribal
> characteristics were lost in a wretched caricature of European methods. There
> is nothing more slovenly than a lithe athletic African dressed in European

---

[4] Fraser, 'Zulu of Nyasaland', 71.

[5] The term **abaZansi** means 'those from the south' (or 'south east') and refers to those Ngoni who came from the Nguni heartland near Lake St. Lucia in what is now KwaZulu.

[6] Fraser, 'Zulu of Nyasaland', 71-72.

[7] Ibid., 73.

cast-off clothing, or more repulsive than a lad trying to be an Englishman
when he should be an Ngoni, proud of his nationality.[8]

He continues that one of the most serious problems facing the missionaries is
how

> to preserve all national customs which are not evil in themselves and yet
> evolve a people honest, industrious, intelligent and Christian, who will have
> some harmonious and beautiful part to take when the world's orchestra is
> filling up to play its symphony of peace and prosperity.[9]

For all the empathetic qualities of the above, Fraser, and those who thought
like him, seemed unaware of the fact that the package of western culture and
economics which the missionaries brought made almost inevitable the very
things which they were trying to prevent.

Fraser's writings on Malawian culture and religion (to which we shall
return later) are not unique. They represent a fairly widespread interest
among several of his colleagues. Apart from Fraser himself (who, as already
indicated, wrote six books and scores of articles) three other Scottish
missionaries might be singled out for mention. W.A. Elmslie, who pre-dated
Fraser working with the Ngoni, published his most famous work, *Among the
Wild Ngoni* in 1899, but also did important early work on the s*i*Ngoni
language and grammar.[10] A.G. Macalpine, though, like Elmslie, coming
from the more theologically conservative wing of the mission, did
considerable serious study of Tonga history and religion. Though he did not
publish any book on the topic, he did produce several articles, which
appeared both in the mission periodical *Aurora* (and, in a slightly different
form in the *Journal of the African Society*).[11] In addition, Macalpine's
papers, in the Special Collections of the University of Edinburgh library,
contain much useful ethnographic material.

On a par with Fraser's productivity, and more important from an
anthropological point of view, was Thomas Cullen Young, who arrived in
Malawi in 1904 (seven years after Fraser) and was much influenced by him
in his comparatively open attitude to African culture. His main work was
amongst the Tumbuka people, and his main works the parallel *Notes on the
Speech and History of the Tumbuka-Henga Peoples*[12] and *Notes on the*

---

[8] Ibid., 75. Here and elsewhere in his writings, Fraser's use of the term 'nationality' might
today better be translated 'ethnicity'.

[9] Ibid.

[10] See, for example, *Izongoma zo'Mlungu*, Blantyre, 1886: probably the first published book
in siNgoni; and *Introductory Grammar of the Ngoni (Zulu) Language*, Aberdeen, 1891.

[11] 'Tonga Religious Beliefs and Customs', *Journal of the African Society*, 1905-06, 1906-07.

[12] Thomas Cullen Young, *Notes on the Speech and History of the Tumbuka-Henga Peoples*,

Customs and Folklore of the Tumbuka-Kamanga Peoples.[13] Though regarding himself as an amateur, Young was undoubtedly a competent anthropologist, becoming a Fellow of the Royal Anthropological Society, and entering into debates in the pages of the publication *Man*. His work has been very adequately covered by Peter Forster, both in his book, *T. Cullen Young: Missionary and Anthropologist*[14] and in his article 'Missionaries and Anthropology: the Case of the Scots of Northern Malawi'.[15] For this reason, and because it is not my primary intention to describe the works of these missionaries, I will make only passing reference to Cullen Young in the rest of this paper.

I want, instead, to look at different ways in which the work of these missionary writers influenced others in their attitudes to African traditional religion and culture. Before doing that, it should be pointed out that the published contribution of Scottish women missionaries in Malawi was very sparse indeed (apart from in-house missionary magazines). The most obvious exception to this was Dr. Agnes Fraser (Donald's wife) who, apart from her biography of Donald Fraser, wrote several pieces and a book on women in Malawi—though concentrating mainly on issues of health and leadership, and saying little about religion.[16]

Apart from the obvious point (already made) that all the missionaries assumed a natural superiority of Christianity over indigenous religion, attitudes towards indigenous religion and culture did tend to vary somewhat between one missionary and another. One general point which might be made was that they tended to look at particular practices, rather than the religion as a whole. And if we, for the sake of clarity, make the somewhat artificial distinction between culture and religion, then it tended to be specific cultural activities—the *mwavi* poison ordeal, polygamy, certain dances considered by the missionaries to be obscene—rather than more narrowly religious rituals, which came in for most missionary criticism. Though it would have to be said that Elmslie, in particular, was critical of traditional rituals for rainmaking, involving sacrificing to the ancestors.[17]

Livingstonia, 1923.

[13] Thomas Cullen Young, *Notes on the Customs and Folklore of the Tumbuka-Kamanga Peoples*, Livingstonia, 1931.

[14] Peter G. Forster, *T. Cullen Young: Missionary and Anthropologist*, Hull, 1989.

[15] Peter G. Forster, in *Journal of Religion in Africa*, 16 (1986), 101-20.

[16] See, for example, Agnes Fraser, *The Teaching of Healthcraft to African Women*, London, 1932; and 'The Neglected Problem of the Women' in *Other Lands*, January 1927, 53-55.

[17] See, for example, Elmslie, *Wild Ngoni*, 168-69.

Speaking of northern Malawi specifically, one might also distinguish between attitudes to the Ngoni, and to surrounding tribes such as the Tumbuka and Tonga. While missionaries working outside the Ngoni area tended to accept the stereotype of the 'Wild Ngoni', those working within *uNgoni* tended to have a much higher view of the morals and culture of the Ngoni, as compared to neighbouring tribes. This is consistent with the common European preference for strong, cattle-keeping, centrally-governed, militaristic peoples such as the Zulu, the Baganda, the Tutsi etc.—a preference which bolstered contemporary European ideas of a hierarchy of races, where some African peoples were regarded as 'superior' to others. Such a view actually helped to create ethnic identity, as in the case of the Tutsi, for example.[18] Thus, in the course of time (as I have pointed out elsewhere) the Ngoni were transformed from 'bloodthirsty savages' into 'stout-hearted Zulus'.[19]

The Scottish missionaries differed in their views as to how far existing religious beliefs and worldviews could be assimilated into Christianity. Most positive were Fraser and Cullen Young; though even they tended to think in terms of general worldview, rather than specific ritual or belief. We should not forget, by the way (though it is not the immediate concern of this paper) that it was the Xhosa missionaries William Koyi and George Williams who first undertook to meet traditional Ngoni concerns over rain and good crops, by going to the chief's kraal to hold special prayer meetings[20]—a tradition built on by Fraser with his huge sacramental conventions, but regarded with suspicion by Elmslie.

How did Scottish missionary views influence others with regard to indigenous religion and culture; and which others did they influence? We could mention briefly four forums where the debate over the relationship between African culture and religion and missionary Christianity was carried on. The first was within the Scottish missionary community in Malawi itself. This happened at two different levels. First at the Livingstonia mission council (made up during this period by the ordained Scottish missionaries and medical doctors)[21] and the Livingstonia Presbytery (a wider body including African representatives, but, in the early years of the century dominated by the Scottish missionaries). A close scrutiny of the minutes of these two bodies shows that, in the early years of the twentieth century a

---

[18] See René Lemarchand, *Ethnicity as Myth: the View from Central Africa*, 1999, 8-12.

[19] See 'Bloodthirsty Savages or Stout-Hearted Zulus?' in this book.

[20] Thompson, *Touching the Heart*, 111-12 & 149-50.

[21] Note that at this period the mission council was an entirely male and European body.

good deal of their time was taken up discussing matters involving African culture. Let us look at just one example—which illustrates both the fact that the missionaries themselves were often split on controversial issues, and also that the few African members of Presbytery were prepared to get involved in the debate.

The custom of *chokoro*—marriage to a dead brother's widow—was a well-established Ngoni custom. It's purpose was two-fold: first to provide a home and security for the widow; secondly to raise up children for the dead brother (since any children born of such a marriage after his death would be regarded as his). Presbytery discussed this issue several times: in May 1900, November 1907, and January 1908. On the last of these occasions the decision of Presbytery was 'that a man may not marry the widow of his deceased brother'.[22] This ruling was obviously not acceptable to many Ngoni Christians, and in October 1911 Loudon kirk session brought forward the issue again. (An indication, by the way, that Donald Fraser, the missionary at Loudon, allowed his Ngoni elders to discuss such matters freely). Some of the more conservative members of Presbytery (including A.G. Macalpine) tried to prevent further discussion of the matter, but Fraser, seconded by Edward Bothi Manda proposed that

> considering that marriage with a deceased brother's widow is common native custom, and is not clearly contrary to Biblical Law, the Presbytery, while discouraging the custom, do not think such a marriage sufficient cause for discipline.[23]

The amendment was carried by nineteen votes to nine, but the following year, while Fraser was in Scotland, the decision was unanimously reversed[24]—probably because the colonial government had warned the mission that they regarded such marriages as illegal under the Native Marriage Ordinance.

There were many other discussions on similar cultural issues, carried on at the different levels of church courts. Such discussions must have helped the missionaries to think more deeply about the African-missionary relationship, though two things need to be said: first, such discussions did not lead to missionary unanimity, but sometimes to deep divisions; secondly, the debate allowed the missionaries (when they were willing to listen) to be informed by the opinions of the African Christians themselves; though here again, opinion was sometimes divided on the African side. Those who were

---

[22] North Livingstonia Presbytery Minutes, 6 November 1907 (quoting 10 May 1900), NAM.

[23] *Ibid.,* 20 October 1911.

[24] *Ibid.,* 18 October 1912.

more outspoken, such as Yesaya Zerenji Mwasi, Edward Bothi Manda and Charles Chinula, often believed that the missionaries were much too negative in their attitudes to African culture, for example on the question of dancing. Once African Christians came to understand that the missionary attitude towards African culture, and particularly anything to do with the ancestral spirits, was predominantly negative, they began to operate a two-tier religiosity, with beliefs and rituals not acceptable to the missionaries sometimes being carried on secretly at grass-roots level. This is particularly the case with regard to funeral rituals

Alongside the discussions of culture and religion within the Livingstonia mission itself, a similar, but wider discussion took place in the regular missionary conferences which were held by the Federated Board of Missions, beginning in 1900, though, as each of the missions remained a separate entity (at least until 1924) such wider discussions did little actually to change thinking within the Livingstonia mission itself.

The part played by Malawian Christians in these discussions is ambivalent. No African Christians were members of either the mission council, or the united missionary conferences. On the other hand, they were members of presbytery, and separate 'native conferences' were often held alongside those of the Federated Missions.

The fourth general missionary conference took place at Livingstonia in September 1924 to coincide with the union of the Blantyre and Livingstonia missions to form the Church of Central Africa, Presbyterian. On this occasion the African clergy present were listed as visitors, and the official report commented that

> The native speakers unanimously emphasized that the Church in Africa has nothing to do with denominational differences of the Home Churches. It finds its base of unity in the Bible.[25]

Nevertheless, the missionary voice remained the dominant discourse during this period, and within the structures of the church African Christians were largely dependant on the goodwill of the more open of the Scottish missionaries to have their voice heard. In one important respect, the comparative openness of missionaries such as Fraser and Cullen Young brought this African voice to a wider audience. This was in the encouragement of a small but significant number of African Christians of the Livingstonia mission to put into writing their own impressions of their cultural and religious heritage. Three examples of this might be mentioned.

---

[25] *Report of the Fourth General Missionary Conference*, 62.

146

The first is the book *Autobiography of an African*[26] (the story of the life of Daniel Nhlane, one of the early Ngoni Christians and evangelists) published under Donald Fraser's name in 1925; the second is Levi Mumba's article 'The Religion of my Fathers'[27] published anonymously in the *International Review of Missions* in 1930, with an introduction by Cullen Young; and the third is Yesaya Chibambo's history of the Ngoni, written originally in chiTumbuka as *Makani gha waNgoni*[28] and later translated by the Scottish missionary Charles Stuart, and published in English as *My Ngoni of Nyasaland*[29] in 1940.

Let me say a little about these three examples of Malawian Christian response on issues of history, culture and religion.[30] First it is possible to interpret the missionary intervention in these works in different ways. On the one hand, had it not been for the interest and encouragement of people like Fraser and Cullen Young, these documents might never have seen the light of day. On the other hand there was clearly a missionary agenda at work here. Steve Chimombo has written in some detail about the way in which Fraser reworked *the Autobiography of an African*,[31] and Cullen Young, in sending Mumba's 'the Religion of my Fathers' to the *IRM* did not reveal the author's name, and, furthermore, wrote a one and a half page introduction in which he warned against the dangers of a Christian mission in which 'Jesus Christ may be preached and taught most earnestly, but not learned'.[32] The article itself is a very low-key description of the traditional religion of northern Malawi in the period before the coming of the missionaries. Mumba himself was an assimilated Ngoni, educated at Livingstonia. He was one of its most influential graduates of the first half of the century, being one of the founders and first secretary in 1912 of the North Nyasa Native Association—the first of a number of such associations, which eventually amalgamated to become the Nyasaland African Congress in 1944, with Mumba as its chairman. He was, however, a suspended member of Livingstonia, and helped to found the African National Church, so his

---

[26] Donald Fraser, *The Autobiography of an African*, London, 1925.
[27] Anonymous [Levi Mumba], 'The Religion of my Fathers', *International Review of Missions*, 19(3), 1930, 362-76.
[28] Yesaya Chibambo, 'Makani gha waNgoni' in *Midauko*, Livingstonia, 1965.
[29] Yesaya Chibambo, *My Ngoni of Nyasaland*, London, n.d. [1940].
[30] For a fuller treatment of this subject, see, 'Speaking for Ourselves: the African Writers of Livingstonia', in this book.
[31] As far as I am aware, this piece, entitled 'Donald Fraser and Autobiography: a Literary History and Travelogue' has not been published.
[32] *International Review of Missions*, 19(3), 1930, 363.

ecclesiastical credit with the Scottish missionaries was less than perfect. As already pointed out, Cullen Young was one of the most liberal and open of the Livingstonia missionaries in his attitude to African religion and customs, but his handling of Mumba's article illustrates, I think, the underlying paradox in much Scottish missionary thinking of the period. Missionaries like Young, Fraser, or even Macalpine could appreciate good elements in both local culture and religion; but their theology never allowed them to see this as anything more than *preparatio evangelium*. A clear example of this theology may be seen in a remark which Fraser made during his 1901 lecture in Glasgow. In a reference to the coronation of the Ngoni paramount Chimtunga, Fraser described how Mpherembe, whom he describes as 'the eldest sub-chief', sacrificed a bull and prayed to the spirit of the dead paramount chief M'mbelwa to bless the new chief. According to Fraser, Mpherembe then continued, 'And O Mombera (*sic*), bless the teachers when they go about teaching the people the words of God.' Fraser then added this comment: 'There was something very beautiful in this recognition of Christianity as but a fuller shining of the dim light they had.'[33] Not all missionaries would have gone even as far as referring to Ngoni religion as a 'dim light'; the 'darkness' motif was very deeply imbedded. And Fraser's formulation that Christianity was '*but* a fuller shining' of traditional religion is not without positive significance.

The third work mentioned above—Yesaya Chibambo's *My Ngoni of Nyasaland*—is, perhaps the least altered by missionary editing. True, it is slightly shorter than the original chiTumbuka version published as *Makani gha waNgoni*, but the omissions make no substantial difference to the overall impact of the work. It was translated into English by the Scottish missionary Charles Stuart, and published in 1940, as the third volume in the 'Africa's Own Library' by the United Society for Christian Literature. Interestingly, the first volume in the series was *My People of Kikuyu* by Jomo Kenyatta. But there is a further interesting point, and that is, by 1940, the Secretary of the United Society for Christian Literature was none other than Thomas Cullen Young, who adds various footnotes to the text.

Though most of the sixty page booklet is concerned with the history and genealogy of the Ngoni there are a few passing references to indigenous religion. Perhaps the most interesting, echoing the missionary theology of *preparatio evangelium*, is the following:

---

[33] Donald Fraser, 'The Zulu of Nyasaland: their Manners and Customs', in *Proceedings of the Philosophical Society of Glasgow*, vol xxxii, 1900-01, 73.

We hear of the prophets of Israel, and the great work that they accomplished. They brought their people into contact with God. But we are apt to forget that God has been slowly revealing himself in every nation of mankind in the world, even among the backward and despised. Every tribe has had its seers who brought the people into contact with the spirits, perhaps we should say, with God. Sometimes they foretold coming events, and sometimes they rebuked the errors of the people.[34]

In looking at this statement by Chibambo, two points need to be borne in mind. First, he recognised value in the traditional religion of his own people; and secondly, he was prepared to compare Ngoni prophets (*izanusi* or *zinchimi*) with the prophets of the Old Testament. Indeed among Christian Ngoni the text of Hebrews 1v.1 was a popular one, 'In the past God spoke to our ancestors many times and in many ways through the prophets, but in these last days he has spoken to us through his Son.'[35]

If I might return briefly to the theme of fulfilment theology, found prominently in the writings of both Fraser and Cullen Young, it is important to recognise that this was not merely a theoretical debate, but had important practical implications in fields such as church discipline. Here one would have to admit that while the group we might call 'the liberals' did from time to time have small victories, overall church discipline and regulations at Livingstonia were dominated by the stricter, less empathetic group, led by figures such as Laws and Elmslie. Apart from the question of specific African cultural practices, this group centred around the extent to which the Presbyterian church in northern Malawi should be a mimetic copy of its Scottish counterpart, and to what extent it should be allowed to develop its own genuinely African characteristics. The struggle is summed up in a dispute which I have dealt with elsewhere,[36] which dragged on for seven years, and which culminated in 1924. The case concerned the suspension, and possible reinstatement of Jonathan Chirwa—one of the first Malawians to have been ordained by the Livingstonia Mission. The details need not concern us here. Suffice it to say that there was a group of missionaries and local Christians willing to reinstate the suspended minister, and another group determined to oppose his reinstatement. At a particularly heated point in the debate (held at a Presbytery meeting in September 1924) those opposed to Chirwa's reinstatement argued that 'it is not church law in

---

[34] Yesaya Chibambo, *My Ngoni*, 52.

[35] Hebrews 1v.1 (Good News Bible: Today's English Version). In the latest version of the chiTumbuka New Testament, *Phangano Lipya*, the word *zinchimi* is used here for 'prophets'.

[36] Thompson, *Christianity*, 204-11. See also 'Donald Fraser and the Ngoni Church' in this volume.

Scotland'. According to my Ngoni informant and friend, Petros Moyo, Fraser countered that ' This is an African church; we cannot take the laws of home.'[37] The point here is that the question of Scottish mission attitudes to African culture and religion was not simply an issue of approaches to particular cultural and religious rituals and practices, but had much wider implications in terms of church discipline, the pace of development of African leadership, and even attitudes to African political advancement.

At the time that the World Missionary Conference was meeting in Edinburgh in 1910, a similar, though much more limited conference was taking place in Malawi. It was the third such conference of the Federated Missions—the major Protestant mission bodies working in the country. Donald Fraser was asked to give a lecture on 'Heathenism'—the negative title itself was indicative of the attitude of most missionaries, and I believe, was not chosen by Donald Fraser himself. Fraser was a skilled communicator, with the ability to begin where his audience were, and lead them to a position where perhaps they did not expect to be. Thus, he began by saying:

> I am not sure how the committee intended this subject to be treated. One might write a depressing enough paper describing the awful sins and errors of heathenism. These are ever before us. But I shall rather spend my time considering some elements in the heathenism we deal with which are avenues towards Christianity.[38]

For the rest of the paper he seldom uses the term 'heathenism', preferring instead the slightly less pejorative 'paganism' or even, 'the religion of the people'. He quotes Biblical verses from both Old and New Testaments to oppose a strict Christian exclusivism which would see no good in other religions. For example, and perhaps somewhat surprisingly, he quotes from Malachi chapter 1, verse 14 to make the point that the Christian God is not opposed to all sacrifice as such, but only to the hypocrisy and lack of sincerity which sometimes accompanies it. He talks with some knowledge about territorial rain shrines in various parts of southern Africa, and speaking of traditional religious practitioners remarks, 'Here are men dedicated to God. Men to whom God gives great and special revelations.'[39] Such a statement might not produce much controversy today, but in the context of European mission to Malawi almost a century ago, it is truly amazing. Not

---

[37] Petros Hlazu Moyo, personal interview, 28 December 1971.

[38] Donald Fraser, 'Heathenism', in *Proceedings of the Third Federated Missions Conference*, Blantyre, 1910.

[39] Ibid.

only does Fraser accept that the God who speaks to Africans *through their traditional religion* is the same God whom the missionaries preach; he also claims that this God actually gives to these 'heathen' practitioners, authentic revelation and knowledge. Fraser goes on to stress the importance of dreams in indigenous cosmologies, and takes issue with Dudley Kidd's assertion that most missionaries do not take them seriously. Speaking of the Christian African and dreams he says, 'If he knows himself to be possessed by God and submits this possession to the test of harmony with the revealed will of God, I do not see why this should not be a great asset to the church'.[40]

Equally important in Fraser's writing, I think, is his willingness to critique various Western attitudes towards Africa and its customs. Taking issue with the widespread Scottish missionary suspicion of the 'emotionalism' of the African, Fraser writes, 'It is not the "canny Scot" but the fervid Celt who is most closely allied to the African',[41] paralleling a phrase he was to use again a few years later, 'We do not want to superimpose on those sons of Africa our expressionless Scottish characters.'[42]

It would, of course, be inaccurate and misleading to imply that there was any sense in which Fraser regarded African indigenous religion as salvifically adequate in itself. He was, after all, among the most enthusiastic of his colleagues for evangelism. There is, nevertheless, both in his very interesting paper on 'Heathenism' and elsewhere in his writings, a clear willingness (to paraphrase the words of George Fox, the founder of the Quakers) to 'refuse light from no quarter': in other words to be open to recognise what was positive and good in any culture or religion.

Whereas Fraser's approach to African culture was indistinguishable from his theological stance, Thomas Cullen Young, as a more accomplished and better read amateur anthropologist, was sometimes willing to put more distance between his own theological views and the anthropological content of much of his writing. To some extent, of course, this was determined by the audience for which he was writing. The subscribers to *Man*, the journal of the Royal Anthropological Society, were less likely to be moved by an appeal to Christian inclusivism than the readers of a church publication such as *Other Lands* might be. As his comments on Levi Mumba's 1930 article 'The Religion of My Fathers' make clear, Cullen Young remained convinced of the superiority of Christianity over indigenous religions; yet at the same

---

[40] Ibid.
[41] Ibid.
[42] Donald Fraser, *Winning a Primitive People*, 287.

time, and perhaps to a greater extent than any of his missionary colleagues he developed for its own sake a genuine and deep interest in the language, culture and history of the Tumbuka people of northern Malawi. Though several of his theories and ideas (for example about patterns of migration and chieftaincy among the Tumbuka) have subsequently been challenged by writers such as Leroy Vail,[43] they nonetheless provided in their time an extremely useful introduction to the topics with which they dealt—not merely for missionaries and mission supporters, but also for those with a more general interest in the area and its peoples.

If we look at the position of the Scottish missionaries in general, however, we are confronted by a paradox. That none of them should think African religion sufficient in itself is hardly surprising; that some of them took fairly negative attitudes towards particular aspects of that spirituality is likewise fairly predictable. What is perhaps more surprising is the considerable amount of material emanating from the Scottish missionaries in northern Malawi which shows empathy with the traditional values of the people among whom they were working. This is particularly true of the work of Donald Fraser and Thomas Cullen Young. Yet there was, even in their work, an unresolved and deep-seated ambiguity. As human beings they had a great deal of respect for the people and culture of the area; as Christian missionaries they believed that the new religion which they brought was superior to that which they found; even though the more sensitive of them were well aware of the fact that the baggage which inevitably accompanied the gospel they carried included many features which would not necessarily benefit the peoples of northern Malawi. It was a paradox which was never satisfactorily resolved.

It is, perhaps, best represented by a sentence in an article written by Donald Fraser in 1908. Within a few months two outstanding old leaders of the Ngoni, Ng'onomo Makamu and *Nkosi* Mabulabo had died. Neither had ever become a Christian, and most missionaries would not even have bothered to record their passing—particularly for an audience in Scotland where the story might seem to indicate missionary failure. Yet Fraser knew and admired them, and wrote an article in the *United Free Church Missionary Record* entitled 'The Passing of two Great Angoni Chiefs'.[44] In it, the following strange but moving sentence occurs: 'to the end they lived

[43] See, for example, Leroy Vail, 'Suggestions Towards a Re-interpreted Tumbuka History' in B. Pachai (Ed.), *The early History of Malawi*, London, 1972.
[44] Donald Fraser, 'The Passing of two Great Angoni Chiefs' in *United Free Church of Scotland Monthly Record*, February 1908, 64.

and died polygamists, drunkards, heathen, yet brave and honourable gentlemen'.[45] It is a sentence which few missionaries could have written with sincerity, as Fraser did; yet it is a sentence which sums up the deeply unresolved ambiguity at the heart of much missionary thinking about African religion and culture.

---

[45] Ibid.

Speaking for Ourselves: the African Writers of Livingstonia[1]

Introduction

When most people think of the writings associated with Livingstonia it is to books such as *Laws of Livingstonia, Among the Wild Ngoni,* or *Winning a Primitive People* that their minds immediately turn. However good some of these writings may be—and their quality varies considerably—concentrating on them has at least two unfortunate side effects. First, it diverts attention from the writings of African authors themselves., and, perhaps even more seriously, it means that, to the outsider, Malawian cultural, religious and political ideas are presented indirectly, through the particular (and inevitably biased) perspective of the European missionary.

A few years ago a group of South African independent church leaders produced a booklet called *Speaking for Ourselves*. In the introduction they had this to say:

> Until now all the research and all the literature about the so-called 'African independent churches' has been the work of outsiders. Anthropologists, sociologists and theologians from foreign churches have been studying us for many years and they have published a whole library of books and articles about us. Each of them has his or her own motives for studying us... It is therefore not surprising that we do not recognise ourselves in their writings.[2]

The purpose of this paper is to allow the Malawian graduates of Livingstonia to 'speak for themselves'. First, to inform those who may not be aware of it (or not *fully* aware of it) of the considerable amount and variety of the published work of those I will call 'Livingstonians', secondly to quote briefly from some of the more interesting publications, and finally, to reflect on the significance of some of the writing and of the missionary interaction with it. Inevitably, in the space available, each of these will have to be done very briefly and inadequately. Again, for reasons of space, I will concentrate

---

[1] An earlier version of this lecture was first delivered at a conference in Edinburgh in 1994, to celebrate the centenary of the moving of the headquarters of the Livingstonia Mission to Khondowe in 1894. It was then published in *Bulletin of the Scottish Institute of Missionary Studies*, New Series 10, 1994, 24-35.

[2] Archbishop N.M. Ngada, *Speaking for Ourselves*, Institute of Contextual Theology, Johannesburg, 1985, 5.

on publications written (though not necessarily published) in the first half of the twentieth century.

Once one begins to look at this subject, the first striking thing is the actual amount of material that has been written by Livingstonians in these years, and the variety of forms and places in which it eventually saw the light of day. Without in any sense claiming to be comprehensive, I will be referring, at least in passing, to the work of at least nine Livingstonians during this period. Such work can be divided into four main categories: first of all, religious work published by, or for, the Livingstonia Synod. Examples of this would be Charles Chinula's translation of *Pilgrim's Progress*,[3] and Samuel Hara's translation of the Old Testament into chiTumbuka.[4] Secondly, work of a more general religious or cultural nature, produced independently of the Livingstonia Mission: examples of this would be Yesaya Chibambo's *My Ngoni of Nyasaland*,[5] and Levi Mumba's 'The Religion of My Fathers', published anonymously in the *International Review of Missions* in 1930.[6] Thirdly, work of a predominantly political character, such as Clements Kadalie's *My Life and the ICU*[7] (to which I will be returning in some detail) written in the late 1940s but not published until 1970, and George Simeon Mwase's *Strike a Blow and Die*,[8] an account of Chilembwe's Rising, written in the early 1930s and published in 1967. Fourthly, articles of a distinctively polemical nature, written against the Livingstonia Mission, or missionaries in general. Into this category would come some of the writings of Charles Domingo for the Seventh Day Baptists—among the earliest published writings by a Livingstonian, beginning around 1910[9]—and Y. Z. Mwasi's *My Essential and Paramount*

---

[3] *Ulendo wa Mukristu mu CiTumbuka*, translated by Charles C. Chinula, Church of Scotland Mission, Livingstonia, 1941.

[4] *Testamente la Kale*, National Bible Society of Scotland, Edinburgh, 1957.

[5] Yesaya M. Chibambo, *My Ngoni of Nyasaland*, Africa's Own Library, No. 3, Heinemann, London, 1940.

[6] [Levi Z. Mumba], 'The Religion of my Fathers', *International Review of Missions*, 19(3), 1930, 362-76.

[7] Clements Kadalie, *My Life and the ICU: the Autobiography of a Black Trade Unionist in South Africa*, London, Frank Cass, 1970.

[8] George Simeon Mwase, *Strike a Blow and Die*, edited with an introduction by Robert Rotberg, Cambridge, Mass., Harvard University Press, 1967.

[9] Many of these are quoted in George Shepperson and Thomas Price, *Independent Africa: John Chilembwe and the Nyasaland Rising of 1915*, Edinburgh, Edinburgh University Press, 1958, especially pages 159-165.

Reasons for Working Independently,[10] first written in 1933, but not finally published until 1979.

Clements Kadalie

Let me begin my survey by looking in some detail at one particular man and his work—and I chose him for two reasons: first, because he is an extremely important figure in the development of black trade unionism in South Africa, and secondly, because, in spite of that he is largely (though not completely) ignored in the Livingstonia 'hall of fame', at least from the missionary perspective. He is Clements Kadalie—born at Chifira village near Bandawe in the mid 1890s—a grandson of chief Chiweyu, and a nephew of both Y. Z. Mwasi and George Simeon Mwase, as well as being related to the Muwamba family. He first went to Khondowe for a continuation class in 1906, returning there in December 1907 to become a boarder. By 1912 he had become (at least by his own account) Dr. Laws' private secretary. As well as training as a teacher he did at least part of the theological course before leaving at the end of 1912 as a qualified teacher. He seems at this point to have been only sixteen or seventeen years old, and rather than being given a school of his own was placed under an older but less qualified teacher with whom he soon quarrelled. Although later given his own school, he left Malawi in 1915 to walk south in search of work..[11] (Not, you may recall, the only subsequently famous product of the Livingstonia Mission to do so at precisely that time).

For the next few years he moved through Mozambique, Zimbabwe and South Africa, filling a number of clerical posts in mines, railways, insurance offices etc. Between 1915 and 1919 he had at least a dozen different jobs. A point of interest to those of us who have taught at Livingstonia is his claim that, because of his general competence and the excellence of his spoken and written English, 'Wherever I was employed I was asked where I had obtained my education.'[12] Though many of Kadalie's statements about his own achievements need to be taken with a pinch of salt, this one seems to ring true. Towards the end of 1918 an incident occurred which was to change his life. In Cape Town he was pushed off the pavement by a white policeman. Kadalie, never one to be intimidated, exclaimed loudly that he

---

[10] Y.Z. Mwasi, *My Essential and Paramount Reasons for Working Independently*, 'Sources for the Study of Religion in Malawi, No. 2, Zomba, Department of Religious Studies, University of Malawi, 1979.

[11] Kadalie, *My Life,*, Chapter 1, 'My Early Life'.

[12] *Ibid.*, p. 35

was going to protest. He was overheard by a European, A. F. Batty, who was about to stand as an Independent Labour candidate in the forthcoming South African elections. Batty said he had witnessed the incident and was willing to back up Kadalie. As a result of this chance encounter Kadalie joined Batty's election committee, and Batty encouraged Kadalie to help form a trade union. On 17th January 1919 the Industrial and Commercial Workers' Union of Africa (more popularly known as the ICU) was formed, and Kadalie, less than twelve months after arriving in South Africa, was elected its secretary.[13]

Several books have been written on the union, and in the space available it would be impossible to do justice to Kadalie's part in its rise (and, unfortunately, its fall). Suffice it to say here that although the ICU was neither the only, nor indeed the first black trade union in South Africa, it did succeed, particularly in the early 1920s, in melding together both black and coloured dock workers and other trades, and, sometimes through direct strike action, in obtaining considerable improvements in their conditions (or at least, if one takes a more pessimistic view, in redressing the fall in living standards in the period after the First World War). Indeed, Kadalie quickly became such a thorn in the flesh of the authorities that in January 1921 (once they had discovered he was from Malawi) he was issued with a deportation order. This was eventually cancelled after representations from several sources—including, according to Kadalie himself 'the Scottish Church'.[14]

By the mid-1920s Kadalie was developing an interesting network of contacts. In 1924 he attended an ANC conference, and soon afterwards met the leading South African politician Hertzog, whom he was encouraging his followers to support in the forthcoming general election, rather than Smuts. It is interesting to note, by the way, that both Kadalie and many of his members had a vote in Cape Province in the 1924 election. By this time he was a well-known figure in many parts of South Africa, and writes that, 'Whenever I travelled by car... teachers would bring to the roadside African schoolchildren waiting for my car, and these would greet me with songs.'[15]

In 1927 Kadalie undertook a European tour which lasted for nearly six months, and included an International Labour Organisation conference in Geneva., an International Trades Union conference in Paris, and visits to Holland, Germany and Austria, as well as two extended visits to Britain. In Britain he was the guest of both the Labour Party and the Independent

[13] *Ibid.*, pp. 39-40
[14] *Ibid.,* pp. 46-47
[15] *Ibid.,* p. 89

Labour Party, addressed meetings at the House of Commons, and travelled to Scotland where he met several ex-Livingstonia missionaries including Donald Fraser and Cullen Young.[16] He was invited to both the United States and the Soviet Union, but in the end was unable to visit either, due to the deterioration in the union's affairs during his absence. But that's another story. For our purposes, Kadalie's importance lies in the fact that in the 1920s he was probably the most important graduate of the Livingstonia system in the first thirty years after the formation of the Overtoun Institution; and that, in addition to his autobiography (which, in fact, was not written to the 1940s) he was regularly in the 1920s a major contributor to the ICU newspaper *the Workers' Herald* as well as contributing occasionally to other periodical, such as *the Messenger* in the USA.

In the same year in which Kadalie toured Europe, Donald Fraser published the last of his six books—*the New Africa*. He chose to begin it with an account of a meeting he had had with Clements Kadalie and another unnamed Malawian ex-soldier at Cape Town docks. Kadalie seems to have been flattered by this passage, for when he came to write his autobiography he chose to quote the passage *verbatim* and without comment. In it Fraser said:

> These lads whom I had just met represented the product of education, but not of mission schools alone. In school they had received their literary education, and their emancipation from their old faith. But since they had left Nyasaland an intensive education had been given them in Flanders and in Cape Town. The things they had seen, the treatment they had received, and the men and women they had met with, had led them a long way... The Scottish missionary who had taught the Trade Union secretary would possibly have been shocked at the idea of native workmen combining to make demands. But this clever lad had gone on to another school, and other teachers had been educating him since he was a pupil in a mission school.[17]

In recognising that the mission education of Livingstonia was only the beginning of a much wider process of maturation in which Livingstonians were hardened and refined in the fields of Flanders and the mines of Witwatersrand, Fraser's ideas were very much in line with those of Kadalie himself. I have discussed Kadalie's career in some detail because, while he is reasonably well known in South Africa (where, however, many people do not realise he was from Malawi) in the story of the Livingstonia Mission I do not believe he has been given the place he deserves. In many respects he is representative of the thousands of Malawians who migrated in search of

---

[16] *Ibid.,* chapter 7, 'My Trip to Europe'.
[17] Donald Fraser, *The New Africa,* London, Church Missionary Society, 1927, p. 10

employment and a better life, and who represented with distinction both their country and the mission which had provided them with an educational start enabling them to shine brightly in a foreign firmament.

A Survey of Livingstonia Writers

Let me now survey briefly some of the publications of Livingstonians in the years between 1900 and the outbreak of the Second World War, before looking finally at some of the lessons to be drawn from a study of these publications.

Among the earliest (and to the missionaries most uncomfortable) of published works by graduates of Livingstonia were the various short pieces to appear in the *African Sabbath Recorder* written by Charles Domingo, who had been brought from Mozambique to Bandawe in 1882 by William Koyi, and who became one of the first graduates of the Livingstonia theological course. After what he considered undue delays in his ordination, and a quarrel with Donald Fraser at Loudon, which the Scottish missionary later regretted, Domingo joined the Seventh Day Baptists, and contributed to their periodicals. While there is probably little of lasting literary value in his writings, he is nevertheless remembered for some of his striking, though ungrammatical phrases. Among the most memorable is his cutting description of the Europeans in Malawi:

> The three combined bodies, Missionaries, Government and Companies, or gainers of money do form the same rule to look upon the natives with mockery eyes… Therefore the life of the three combined bodies is altogether too cheaty, too thefty, too mockery.[18]

Of more significance, perhaps, was the autobiography of Daniel Mtusu Nhlane—only partially completed when he died in 1917. It was completed by his friend Andrew Mkochi, and then translated into English and re-worked by Donald Fraser before being published as *Autobiography of an African*[19] in 1925.

While Daniel Nhlane's story has some importance in setting his own personal story in the wider historical context of northern Malawi in the late nineteenth century, Yesaya Chibambo's *Makani gha waNgoni* is much more significant in attempting a comprehensive history of the northern Ngoni from their origins in South Africa to their settlement in Malawi and the

---

[18] Quoted in Shepperson and Price, *Independent African*, p. 163
[19] Donald Fraser, *Autobiography of an African: Retold in Biographical Form and in the Wild African Setting of the Life of Daniel Mtusu*, London, Seeley, Service and Company., 1925

coming of the Livingstonia Mission. In 1940, having been translated by Charles Stuart, it appeared in English as *My Ngoni of Nyasaland*[20] in the series *Africa's Own Library*—the first of which had been Jomo Kenyatta's *My People of Kikuyu*. In 1930 Levi Mumba became the first Livingstonian (as far as I am aware) to have an article published in a prestigious international journal, when 'The Religion of My Fathers' appeared in the *International Review of Missions*.[21] The fact that the article appeared anonymously is a curiosity to which we shall return later.

At much the same time Samuel Hara—a schoolteacher from Mzimba, then working at Chipata in Zambia—was in the middle of a Herculean task: the single-handed translation of the Old Testament into chiTumbuka. In the second half of 1930 he wrote to Donald Fraser in Glasgow informing him of his intentions. Fraser clearly thought the task was beyond him, but wrote back an encouraging letter urging him to persevere in the hope that his work might be of use to future translators.[22]

Samuel Hara movingly but matter-of-factly tells the story from his perspective in the Introduction to the *Testamente la Kale*, eventually published in 1957:

> In the month of July 1928 I began thinking about my father's respect name... This gave birth in my heart to the desire that I should start translating the Old Testament into Tumbuka, even though I have neither wisdom or intelligence, nor knowledge of Hebrew, Latin or Greek. On 27 March 1930 I began struggling with this frightening, important and difficult task; and I, without qualification, who am rubbish, fit for the pit, muddy water left over from brick-making, who should not even have begun the work, did begin it, and on 15 October 1933 I finished it. Hallelujah![23]

The 'Hallelujah' is Hara's; but it might well be ours also.

I was interested to note during visits to Malawi in the 1980s and 1990s that although there has been a very thorough new translation of the Tumbuka Bible, many people were still using Samuel Hara's translation, more than sixty years after he completed it.

---

[20] See note 5 above.

[21] See note 6 above.

[22] Donald Fraser to Samuel Hara, 8th October 1930, Livingstonia Papers, National Library of Scotland, Ms. 7690.

[23] Maronje [Introduction], Tumbuka Old Testament, Edinburgh, National Bible Society of Scotland, 1957. Though the final English translation is mine, I am grateful to Rev. Jacob Kumwenda for help in unravelling some of the more difficult chiTumbuka phrases.

Patterns in the Publications

The above is merely a very brief and incomplete survey of the writings of Livingstonians in the first half of the twentieth century. What can we learn from a study of publications such as these about the development both of a religious and political consciousness among Livingstonians during this period? Below I highlight ten points, and comment briefly on each.

First, Livingstonia education encouraged students to express themselves both orally and in writing. Two examples from 1904 and 1905 (just ten years after the move to Khondowe) will suffice. The first was a debate on tribal excellency held at the Institution Literary Society. A contemporary report of the debate makes it clear that this was far from being a sectarian affair, but rather an attempt at a rational defence of cultural practices.[24] The second was the beginning of the publication of *Makani*, a vernacular periodical, edited by Fraser, but encouraging contributions by Livingstonians.[25]

Secondly, underpinning the fairly extensive corpus of actual publications was a much more extensive library of unpublished correspondence, some of which has considerable historical importance in its own right. Let me take two examples. The first is a letter of protest against conditions of mission employment, written to Mission Council by Yesaya Chibambo in 1921. I would like to be able to quote this letter in full,[26] with its many insights into the frustrations of local teachers and ministers working for the mission; but space limits us to a few extracts from it.

> There is a great fear on the part of the native to write to the masters or officials, and such fear conceals much of his thought from the mind of the European.
>
> No native is allowed to report about his own work... The report which comes to Mission Council from a native is only taken through a missionary; [This letter itself from Chibambo was presented by Elmslie] and sometimes the missionary who writes the same report does not understand really about the work done by the native. This is especially the case where the missionary holds a temporary place.
>
> The missionary is in Africa for the uplift and improvement of the native. This improvement can better be carried out if the mind of the native and the missionary are working and designing together.

---

[24] *Missionary Record of the United Free Church of Scotland*, October 1904, p. 481

[25] The first issue appeared on 15th March 1905

[26] Following my highlighting this letter and its historical importance, it was published in full in Kenneth R Ross (Ed.), *Christianity in Malawi: a Source Book*, Gweru, Mambo-Kachere, 1996.

One feels therefore, that it is now time when some of the more remarkable native servants of the mission should be encouraged to attend the Mission Council. If the work of the missionary is to be complete in Africa he will seek harmony with the native mind and try to develop it.[27]

Though the Mission Council spent considerable time discussing and replying to Chibambo's points, they conceded few of them—arguing, for example, that it was much too soon to consider African representation on the Mission Council. It was, after all, only in the previous year that the first European woman had been admitted. Yet in the same year that Chibambo protested in Malawi, in another area of the United Free Church of Scotland's work, four local Christians were admitted to the UFC East Himalayan Mission Council, proving that such inclusion was possible.[28]

Now a second example of a large body of important but unpublished material written by Livingstonians during these years. There exists a considerable amount of correspondence from Clements Kadalie, scattered between the National Archives of Malawi, several archives in South Africa, and (somewhat unexpectedly) the public library of Kingston upon Hull in the north east of England.[29] Much of this forms a background to Malawian opinion on political and economic development of the time, and remains an important historical source today.

Thirdly, the actual publications of Livingstonia graduates were more widespread than might be imagined—appearing more often outside Malawi than within, and being scattered in South Africa, the United Kingdom and the USA. The English translation of Yesaya Chibambo's *Makani gha waNgoni*, for example, appeared in the *Africa's Own Library* series, published by the United Society for Christian Literature in London, while George Simeon Mwase's account of the Chilembwe Rising, *Strike a Blow and Die* (probably recorded from Wallace Kampingo, who took part in the Rising, while they were both together in Zomba prison)[30] was first published in the USA.

Fourthly, the position of the missionaries in this process was ambivalent. On the one hand they were often supportive—Donald Fraser encouraging

---

[27] Livingstonia Mission Council Minutes, July 1921, Appendix to Minute 26, National Archives of Malawi

[28] Cindy Perry, 'The History of the Expansion of Protestant Christianity among the Nepali Diaspora', unpublished PhD thesis, University of Edinburgh, 1994, p. 84

[29] Kadalie's letters in the Kingston upon Hull library are from the collected papers of Winifred Holtby, with whom he corresponded.

[30] This is the opinion of Robert Rotberg in his introduction to *Strike a Blow and Die*, pp.xxix-xxx

Daniel Nhlane to write down the story of his life, Cullen Young sending Levi Mumba's article on 'the Religion of My Fathers' to the *International Review of Missions*, Charles Stuart translating Chibambo's *Makani gha waNgoni* to become *My Ngoni of Nyasaland*. On the other hand, such publications were often manipulated by the missionaries for their own purposes. Steve Chimombo has written extensively on Fraser's re-working of the *Autobiography of an African*,[31] for example; but an even more interesting example is the way in which Cullen Young handled Levi Mumba's article. When it appeared in the *International Review of Missions* in 1930 there was no sign of the author's name. Instead a one and a half page introduction by Cullen Young began 'the following article is the work of a member of one of the Nyasaland tribes';[32] but the author is nowhere identified. The 'Notes on Contributors' for that issue say 'The anonymous article "The Religion of My Fathers" was furnished to us by Rev. T. Cullen Young, of the Livingstonia Mission of the Church of Scotland, who guarantees its authenticity.'[33] This would seem to indicate that it was Cullen Young's decision to publish the article anonymously. Again, in the index to the *IRM* for 1930 the article is described as being 'anonymous'.[34] Cullen Young uses his introduction to the article to warn against the dangers of a Christian mission in which 'Jesus Christ may be preached and taught most earnestly, but not learned'.[35] What was an honest and straightforward account of African traditional religion had become a stick with which to beat (albeit fairly gently) the suspended Levi Mumba, and others like him, who upheld the values of traditional customs and beliefs.

One might also comment very briefly on the fact that missionary translation or editing of the works of Livingstonians was sometimes resented. The most eloquent outburst of such resentment comes in a letter from Charles Chinula to W.H. Watson, concerning Chinula's translation of *Pilgrim's Progress* into chiTumbuka. Chinula, who by this time had broken away to form his own church, objected to the fact that Cullen Young had edited his translation. He wrote:

---

[31] Steve Chimombo, 'Donald Fraser and Autobiography: a Literary History and Travelogue'. As far as I am aware, this typescript has never been published.
[32] *International Review of Missions*, 19(3), 1930, p. 362
[33] *Ibid.*, p. 472
[34] *Ibid.*, p. 640
[35] *Ibid.*, p. 363

Mr. C. Young believed himself to have mastered ciTumbuka but made some changes in my translations. It would be absurd for me to try to correct an English book written by a white man.[36]

Another aspect of this ambivalent missionary involvement was the fact that, at least for those still working for the mission, and certainly for those hoping to publish within Malawi, the whole process of publication was controlled by the missionaries. On the one hand, of course, missionary encouragement often led to the appearance of publications which would not otherwise have seen the light of day, on the other hand, the missionaries had their own agendas, as we have seen with Cullen Young's part in the publication of *the Religion of My Fathers*. Furthermore, where missionary patronage was missing, for example in the case of Y.Z. Mwasi's important though critical text explaining his break with the Livingstonia mission, publication could be denied or long delayed. The story of the eventual publication of *My Essential and Paramount Reasons for Working Independently*[37] is worth telling briefly, since it illustrates the circuitous routes by which some of these publications eventually appeared in print. John Parratt, then Professor of Religious Studies at the University of Malawi, had already come across a typescript copy of Mwasi's text, but wasn't sure how accurate it was. While searching through a furniture store-room on the Blantyre mission, Jim Campbell (then a tutor at Kapeni Theological College) found what appeared to be a manuscript version of the document. He passed this on to me, since I was working on various letters of Mwasi at the time, and was familiar with his handwriting. I was able to verify that the document was, in fact, written in Mwasi's own hand-writing. We passed it on to John Parratt who was then able to publish a typescript form of what, in its own way, is one of the most interesting and important documents to have come out of the entire church history of Malawi. Subsequently, of course, the document was re-published by Kachere Press.[38]

Fifthly, and regrettably, the publications of Livingstonians were almost exclusively male. When one looks at the missionary counterparts of the publications we are discussing in this paper, the same pattern of male preponderance applies, so perhaps it is not surprising that Malawian women are almost entirely absent from the publication scene at this period. There are, as far as I am aware, only two limited exceptions—the single hymn of

---

[36] Charles C. Chinula to W.H. Watson, 1st August 1941. Original held by T. Jack Thompson

[37] See note 10, above.

[38] Y.Z. Mwasi, *Essential and Paramount Reasons for Working Independently*, Blantyre, Christian Literature Association in Malawi, 1999.

Jessie Nyagondwe in *Sumu za Ukristu,*[39] and possibly (and I have not been able to check this) a few contributions by women to the vernacular versions of *Makani*, and later, *Vyaru na Vyaru.*

In tribute to the apparently silent women of Malawi, let me at least quote the following account from the Girls' Logbook of the Livingstonia Institution for 2nd July 1897, which indicates quite clearly that while female Livingstonians may have been largely denied the opportunity to go into print, they were more than able to express their views clearly and forcefully:

> This week there has been a rebellion amongst the Ngoni girls. Owing to the cold they refused to begin work at the usual hour in the morning and consequently upset arrangements for the day. They objected also to their bath, even at mid-day. When reasoned with most gave in, but five said they would go home rather than submit to the rules. The five were Helen Bangiwe, Elizabeth Jere, Maggie Cabiri Jere, Martha Loziriro and Jane Kadwaya. They were called in one by one, to state their grievances to Dr. Laws, and were shown by him that they could not go home with credit to themselves, to their relations, nor to their teachers. Finally they agreed to come under discipline, and were met half-way by an arrangement which allowed them to start work half an hour later during the cold weeks.[40]

Sixthly, the Livingstonians who were writing material in the years prior to the Second World War were open to a wide range of outside literary influences. To mention but one, several Malawians, including Y.Z. Mwasi, had access to Marcus Garvey's *Negro World*—a publication regarded as so seditious by the colonial authorities that it was for some time banned in Central Africa, and at least one early leader of the Nyasaland African Congress was imprisoned for possessing a copy.[41]

On the other hand, and seventhly, most of the Livingstonian writers, including those producing secular works such as Kadalie's autobiography, were steeped in imagery from the Bible and from European church history, and quoted both sources frequently in their works. Thus Mwasi, in his *Essential and Paramount Reasons for Working Independently* writes: 'In each country there must be a Moses, a Luther, a Calvin, a Knox etc This is the natural law and this is Divine arrangement';[42] while Charles Chinula in his letter to Willie Watson says: 'We don't care of what man says, for so it was with Luther, John Knox, Dr. Chalmers etc.'[43]

---

[39] Sumu 332, 'Rekani kusuzgika na vintu vya pa caru'
[40] Overtoun Institution, Girl's Log Book, held at Livingstonia Secondary School.
[41] Robert I. Rotberg, *The Rise of Nationalism in Central Africa: the Making of Malawi and Zambia, 1873-1964*, Cambridge, Massachusetts, Harvard University Press, 1965, p. 183.
[42] Mwasi, *Essential and Paramount Reasons,* p. 2.
[43] Charles Chinula to W.H. Watson, 1st August 1940; original held by T Jack Thompson.

But eighthly, many of these writers moved beyond the Biblical and historical analogies with which they had been imbued at Livingstonia, to new and interesting insights of their own. Here again is Kadalie, writing of his first impressions of London in 1927:

> No bigger contrast could be imagined than the contrast between the squalid streets of the East End and the scene in Hyde Park, no more than a couple of miles away. Here one realised Hyde Park as nothing more than a bad joke, a sort of by-product of civilisation, and knew that these poverty stricken streets, stunted and pathetic human beings, the great factory chimneys, which rose to the sky, and the queer, uncouth foreign sailors who slouched by one, were the bedrock and reality on which western civilisation was built. Western civilisation has accomplished things of infinite magnitude. It has built great bridges and machines and spanned the world with steamships and railroads. It has awakened in mankind the thirst for knowledge and power, and it has planned and foretold the course of the stars. But still it has not learned that while great masses of its children go hungry and barefoot, and while the very thirst for knowledge which it has itself awakened is stunted and denied to a large proportion of its men and women, it carries its own failure inherent within itself. All these things are to be learned as well in the East End of London as in the slums of Johannesburg and in the poverty and squalor in which African workers are forced to live.[44]

One can detect a strong sense of irony in this passage, as Kadalie turns back on Europe the intellectual and cultural magnifying glass with which Europeans had so recently examined Africa, and (from their perspective) found it wanting.

Ninethly, and sadly, much of the best of this writing came from those who had, for one reason or another, severed their links with the Livingstonia mission. It seems that the need to toe the party line (and I use this expression deliberately) inhibited the literary creativity and forthrightness of expression of most of those still working for the mission.

And finally, there is present in much of the writing of these Livingstonians a burning desire to put the African side of the case. Let us look briefly at two of many examples. The first section of Y.Z. Mwasi's *My Essential and Paramount Reasons for Working Independently* is a passionate plea for a more African understanding of Christianity. We can quote only a part of it here:

> I wish to save my fellow natives from or to detract their mind from the erroneous idea that God is more in foreign missionaries, lands, languages, institutions, thoughts, words and actions, but is less or not in the native Christianity, languages, institutions, thoughts, words and actions: that God

---

[44] Kadalie, *My Life and the ICU,* p. 115.

loves white colour and hates black colour. In short, that [a] white man, on account of his good surroundings is nearer God than a black man who lacks such environments. That is, another man's God, faith, thought or actions have no personal appeal to me, nor are my personal properties or virtues. Real and personal Christianity of the soil shall begin in members of the native churches when they believe in *an indigenous and personal God*, who is with them, with their native agents, in their country, hearts, thoughts and words and actions in the truest sense as He is with some other races.[45]

Clements Kadalie put the case equally forcibly from a political point of view when he wrote to Isa Macdonald Lawrence in 1925 asking for more information on John Chilembwe, because, as he said, 'I believe the white man will not preserve the genuine history of the black man'.[46] Such a view, which may have been regarded as shocking or even seditious by many Europeans at the time, would now be regarded as orthodox and self-evident by most historians of Africa today.

Kadalie's concern, like that of Y.Z. Mwasi, George Simeon Mwase, Yesaya Chibambo and many other Livingstonians of the time, was to be able to tell their own story in their own way. They wanted simply to be able to speak for themselves. That they were able to do so with such eloquence and persuasiveness is a tribute, not only to the education they received at Livingstonia, but also to their own character, intelligence and determination.

---

[45] Mwasi, *My Essential and Paramount Reasons,* p. 1.
[46] Clements Kadalie to Isa Macdonald Lawrence, 4th April 1925, National Archives of Malawi, Zomba, Ms. 2/28/21

Selected Bibliography

The following bibliography contains the most frequently used sources in these essays.

Archives

National Library of Scotland (NLS)

Livingstonia Papers

National Archives of Malawi (NAM)

Livingstonia Papers

National Archives of United Kingdom (NAUK)

Colonial Office Papers (File 525)

Edinburgh University Library, Special Collections (EUL)

Dr. Laws' Papers
Rev. A.G. Macalpine Papers
Shepperson Collection

Cory Library, Rhodes University, Grahamstown

Lovedale Papers
Roberts' Papers

Personal Interviews

Mtonga, Mbalo, deceased CCAP minister
Moyo, Petros H, deceased Ngoni historian
Taylor, Helen, deceased Scottish missionary
Watson, W.H., deceased Scottish missionary

Journals and Newspapers

Aurora
Central African Times
Christian Express
Free Church of Scotland Monthly
Lovedale News
Scots Observer
United Free Church of Scotland Missionary Record

Published Books and Articles

Bryant, A.T., *Zulu People*, Pietermaritzburg, Shuter and Shooter, 1949.

Chibambo, Yesaya M, *My Ngoni of Nyasaland*, London, Heinemann, 1940.

Chibambo, Yesaya M., 'Makani gha waNgoni' in *Midauko*, Blantyre, Livingstonia Synod, 1965, 51-87.

Colvin, Tom, (Editor), *Come Let us Walk this Road Together*, Carol Stream, Illinois, Hope Publishing Company, 1997.

De Kock, Leon, *Civilising Barbarians*, Johannesburg, Witwatersrand University Press, 1996.

Döhne, J.L., *A Zulu-Kafir Dictionary*, Cape Town, G.J. Pike, 1857.

Elmslie, Walter Angus, *Izongoma zo Mlungu*, Blantyre, Blantyre Mission Press, 1886

Elmslie, Walter Angus, *Among the Wild Angoni*, Edinburgh, Oliphant, Anderson and Ferrier, 1899.

Forster, Peter G., *T Cullen Young: Missionary and Anthropologist*, Hull, Hull University Press, 1989.

Fraser, Agnes, *The Teaching of Healthcraft to African Women*, London, 1932.

Fraser, Agnes, *Donald Fraser of Livingstonia*, London, Hodder & Stoughton, 1934.

Fraser, Donald, 'The Zulu of Nyasaland: their Manners and Customs' in *Proceedings of the Philosophical Society of Glasgow*, Vol. xxxii, 1900-1901, 60-75.

Fraser, Donald, *Winning a Primitive People*, London, Seeley Service, 1914.

Fraser, Donald, *Livingstonia: the Story of our Mission*, Edinburgh, United Free Church of Scotland, 1915.

Fraser, Donald, *Autobiography of an African*, London, 1925.

Fraser, Donald, *The New Africa*, London, Church Missionary Society, 1927.

Fraser, Donald, 'The Evangelistic Approach to the African' in *International Review of Missions*, XV (1926), 438-49.

Hamilton, Carolyn (Ed.), *The Mfecane Aftermath*, Johannesburg, Witwatersrand University Press, 1995.

Jack J.W., *Daybreak in Livingstonia*, Edinburgh, Oliphant, Anderson and Ferrier, 1901.

Kadalie, Clements, *My Life and the ICU*, London, Frank Cass, 1970.

Labuschagne, A.S., *The Missionary*, Bloemfontein, Self-published, 2002.

Laws, Robert, *Reminiscences of Livingstonia*, Edinburgh, Oliver and Boyd, 1934.

Lemarchand, René, *Ethnicity as Myth: the View from Central Africa*, Occasional Paper, Centre of African Studies, University of Copenhagen, 1999.

Livingstone, David and Charles, *Narrative of an Expedition to the Zambezi and its Tributaries*, London, John Murray, 1865.

Livingstone, W. P., *Laws of Livingstonia*, London, Hodder & Stoughton, n.d., [1921].

Lovedale Past and Present: a Record of Two Thousand Names, Lovedale, Lovedale Press, 1887.

Macalpine, A.G., 'Tonga Religious Beliefs and Customs', *Journal of the African Society*, 1905-06, 1906-07.

McCracken, J., *Politics and Christianity in Malawi*, Cambridge, Cambridge University Press, 1977. Reprinted with a new Introduction: Blantyre, CLAIM-Kachere, 2000.

McCracken, John, 'Underdevelopment in Malawi: the Missionary Contribution', in *African Affairs*, 76, 1977.

McLynn, Frank, *Stanley: the Making of an African Explorer*, Chelsea, MI, Scarborough House, 1990

Morrison, J.H., *Forty Years in Darkest Africa*, Edinburgh, United Free Church, 1917.

Mumba, Levi Z, 'The Religion of My Fathers' in *International Review of Missions*, 19(3), 1930, 362-76.

Mwase, George Simeon, *Strike a Blow and Die*, Cambridge Massachusetts, Harvard University Press, 1967.

Mwasi, Y.Z., *My Essential and Paramount Reasons for Working Independently*, Blantyre, CLAIM-Kachere, 1979.

Ngada, N.M., *Speaking for Ourselves*, Johannesburg, Institute of Contextual Theology, 1985.

Pachai, Bridglal, *The Early History of Malawi*, London, Heinemann, 1972.

Read, Margaret, *The Ngoni of Nyasaland*, London, Oxford University Press, 1956.

Read, Margaret, 'Songs of the Ngoni People' in *Bantu Studies*, 11(1), 1937.

Roberts, Andrew, *A History of the Bemba*, London, Longmans, 1973.

Ross, Andrew, *Blantyre Mission and the Making of Modern Malawi*, Blantyre, CLAIM-Kachere, 1996.

Rotberg, Robert I., *The Rise of Nationalism in Central Africa*, Cambridge, Mass., Harvard University Press, 1965.

Shepherd, R. H.W., *Lovedale South Africa 1841-1941*, Lovedale, Lovedale Press, n.d. [1941]

Shepherd, R.H.W. *Lovedale South Africa 1824-1955*, Lovedale, Lovedale Press, 1955.

Shepperson George and Price Thomas, *Independent African*, Edinburgh, EUP, 1958.

Stewart, James, *Livingstonia: its Origin*, Edinburgh, Andrew Elliot, 1894.

Stewart, James, *Lovedale South Africa: Illustrated with Fifty Views from Photographs*, Edinburgh, Andrew Elliot, 1894.

Thompson, T. Jack (Ed.), *From Nyassa to Tanganyika: the Journal of James Stewart C.E. in Central Africa, 1876-1879*, Blantyre, Central Africana, 1989.

Thompson, T. Jack, *Christianity in Northern Malawi: Donald Fraser's Missionary Methods and Ngoni Culture*, Leiden and New York, E. J. Brill, 1995.

Thompson, T. Jack, *Touching the Heart: Xhosa Missionaries to Malawi 1876-1888*, Pretoria, University of South Africa Press, 2000.

Wallis, J.P.R., *The Zambesi Journal of James Stewart*, London, 1952.

Wells, James, *Stewart of Lovedale: the Life of James Stewart*, London, Hodder & Stoughton, 1909.

Young, E.D., *Nyassa: A Journal of Adventures*, London, John Murray, 1877.

Young, Thomas Cullen, *Notes on the Customs and Folklore of the Tumbuka-Kamanga Peoples*, Livingstonia, Livingstonia Mission, 1931.

www.ingramcontent.com/pod-product-compliance
Lightning Source LLC
Chambersburg PA
CBHW021829020426
42334CB00014B/545